KEEPING *A* HEAD IN SCHOOL

KEEPING *A* HEAD IN SCHOOL

A Student's Book about Learning Abilities and Learning Disorders

Dr. Mel Levine

Educators Publishing Service, Inc.
Cambridge and Toronto

Illustrations by Anne Lord and Ann Jennings
Cover design by Hugh Price
Text design by Joyce C. Weston

ISBN 0-8388-2069-7

Educators Publishing Service, Inc., 75 Moulton Street, Cambridge, MA 02138-1104

To my patients, who have taught me almost
all that I have ever needed to know about
learning disorders.

Contents

Acknowledgments

Many fine people contributed to the making of this book. I would like to thank Martha Reed for her many suggestions and for helping us find some interesting writing samples. Mary May of Educators Publishing Service did a superb job of editing, helping to rethink and reorganize various chapters, and dealing with important details that would have been missed because of the author's attentional limitations. I am grateful to Barbara Cassell for her help in typing early versions of the manuscript and to Barbara Levine for her meticulous review of the text. My appreciation extends also to the Geraldine R. Dodge Foundation and to Scott McVay, its Executive Director, for their generous support in helping me and my colleagues work with the age group for whom this book is primarily intended. Finally, I would like to thank all of the animals on my farm for entertaining me while I was writing these chapters.

Introduction for Parents, Teachers, and Other Interested Adults*

The Book's Purpose: *Keeping A Head in School* is a book whose purpose is to prevent harmful misunderstandings about learning disorders.** Reflecting the author's two decades of work evaluating children with learning disorders, the book aims primarily to help such children gain a realistic insight into their personal strengths and weaknesses. It aims also to clarify for them the struggles that may beset them in school. Such information should help students with learning disorders feel more comfortable and more competent.

The ideas in these pages combine candor and realism with justifiable optimism so that a student's enhanced insight into his or her learning disorders (and strengths) will engender hopefulness and ambition. Students may then believe that the struggle to learn is worth the effort, that ultimately it will be rewarding.

Most of all, *Keeping A Head in School* is intended to help children feel that they have efficacy. These pages attempt to empower students with learning disorders to advocate for themselves, to see themselves as resilient beings, to use adults effectively as resources, to deploy their strengths, and to preserve and cherish their own individuality.

Youngsters with learning disorders are frequently so disappointing to themselves, their parents, and their teachers. Their plight is unduly sad, in part because they face needless embarrassment and agonizing confusion. In fact, very few students with learning disorders under-

---

*Kids can read this introduction, too, if they want to. If they do, they should know that the language in this section is much more difficult than it is in the rest of the book, which has been written especially for younger readers.

**Throughout this book, the term *learning disorders* is used rather than the term *learning disabilities*. The reason for this is that, in many communities, learning disabilities are defined specifically by discrepancies between intelligence and achievement tests. However, the subject matter of this book is broader, covering a wide range of learning difficulties that may or may not result in such discrepancies.

stand their learning disorders. This widespread lack of insight is not only striking but also alarming. It is highly unlikely that a child with learning disorders will be able to deal optimally with a condition that is obscure to him or her.

What's more, many children develop false notions about their learning problems, and these misconceptions are often far worse than the problems themselves. The false notions may lead to a profound sense of helplessness, a feeling of being out of control of one's academic destiny. Often students with learning disorders come to believe that they are somehow pervasively and hopelessly defective. They may even articulate the possibility that people are trying to protect or shield them from the truth with terms such as *learning disability*, *dyslexia*, or *attention deficit disorder*. Many youngsters interpret these labels as polite ways of describing a brain that is wholly inadequate.

Some students vacillate between believing that they are retarded and feeling that there is absolutely nothing wrong with them. They further speculate that if there is nothing wrong with them, then they are certainly "losers," since someone who is "normal" should be able to do well in school. Such a sense of being a loser can induce feelings of futility and needless guilt. Students with learning disorders need to recognize that they are neither pervasively defective nor perfectly normal. Furthermore, they need to discover that we all harbor imperfections, that no brain is completely free from flaws!

The Title: At least two messages are implicit in the title *Keeping A Head in School*. The first is that, even when a school experience is somewhat adverse, a student must strive to "keep a head"—his or her head— in school; that is, not to give up, not to come to school with a vigorous body and a head that has needlessly resigned itself to failure, sapped of the energy needed to strive and succeed. The second message is that students should realize that there are many ways to "keep ahead" in school. Even in the face of learning disorders, a student should find reasons to feel that he or she can be ahead —in motivation, in optimism, in the development of outside interests, and in various other ways.

The Intended Audience: This book has been written with adolescents and preadolescents in mind. Much of the language has been calibrated to that age group. However, it is likely that both younger and older students can benefit from exposure to its contents. Some younger students may need to have portions of the book read to them. Older students should not find it too juvenile. In any case, many who read this book will recognize aspects of their own learning styles described in various chapters. Students will likely recognize specific personal strengths as well as one or more of their dysfunctions.

The Book on Tape: *Keeping A Head in School* is also available on a set of tape cassettes, with the author reading the text of the book verbatim. Some students may want to listen to a tape as they read the same material.

Uses: Ideally, children who read this book will talk about it with an adult. A parent, clinician, or teacher can read the book before or after the child does so. There can be discussion of the case vignette presented at the beginning of most chapters, or, alternatively, there can be discussion about the student who has read the material and how it is or is not relevant to him or her. This book can also be used in a special education program; that is, all students within the program can read and discuss its contents with a special education teacher leading the discussions. In clinical settings, it can be read and reviewed as a means of enhancing personal insight. For example, as part of counseling, a student may be asked to read a particular chapter or chapters so that relevant content may be used as a basis for sharing and exploring ideas about the student's experiences in school.

Keeping A Head in School may also be of interest to children without learning disorders. It can be a resource in a course on health, development, or psychology in a secondary school. The book might be read by siblings or friends of children who have learning disorders. Brothers and sisters, in particular, need an understanding of the issues associated with impaired school performance in a sibling.

Contents: *Keeping A Head in School* consists of several sections. The first chapter deals with some basic concepts related to learning disorders. It stresses the fact that learning disorders represent variations in brain function that affect performance in school. It emphasizes that there are many types of learning disorders and that students with these problems need to understand themselves and be understood by the adults in their lives. The first chapter also includes some discussion of normal brain function.

Chapters 2 through 5 cover specific developmental functions such as attention, language, and memory. In each of these chapters there is a presentation of normal brain function and the ways in which variations in function comprise distinct learning disorders. These chapters are *not* intended to help students diagnose themselves. Instead, they are intended simply to portray the wide gamut of possible learning disorders and their impacts.

Chapter 6 reviews the four basic skills areas: reading, spelling, writing, and math. It attempts to relate performance in these areas to the various developmental functions and learning disorders described in the previous chapters.

Chapter 7 deals specifically with social skills since many students with learning disorders experience social stress in school. This association of social skills with learning disorders encourages students to believe that one can *become* skilled socially, just as one can improve skills in reading and other academic areas. This chapter also stresses the importance of not over-relying on social gratification in school.

The next chapter, 8, contains a series of questions that students have about learning disorders. These questions and answers to them are presented to demystify some commonly used labels, diagnostic procedures, and services. Reading this chapter should encourage students to pose additional questions about learning disorders. Such questions can lead to fertile discussions and to the compilation of appropriate answers. In a sense, this chapter stimulates students to question what is happening to them so that they do not settle for a confused or incomplete picture of what is occurring in their lives at school.

The 9th and final chapter, which relates to the future, has two basic objectives. First, it attempts to leave the reader feeling optimistic about what's ahead. Second, it aims to demonstrate to the student that there is much he or she can do to overcome or circumvent learning disorders. Neither this chapter, nor the book in general, is intended to suggest a "cure" or to offer a comprehensive set of recommendations for the management of learning disorders. There is, however, in this final chapter a sampling of possible actions that a student can take in order to minimize the long range effects of learning disorders.

CHAPTER ONE

Learning Disorders and the Human Brain

THE IMPORTANCE OF SUCCESS

Success is like a vitamin. Everyone needs some of it. When you don't have enough success, it's hard to feel very good about who you are, especially when other people around you seem to have plenty of success. When you're growing up, school is the place where you learn the most about success—what it is, how to find it, and how much of it you usually have. You can tell how successful you are just about every day in school. You compare yourself to other kids, and other kids compare themselves to you. If you learn quickly and easily, if you are good at pleasing your teachers and your parents, if you feel as capable as other students, school can be a great experience. But for some kids, school is no fun because they have trouble succeeding, and they just don't feel good about learning.

THE IMPORTANCE OF KEEPING AHEAD IN SCHOOL

Often students who are doing poorly in school subjects come to feel that they are behind in everything. They don't realize that there are many ways to "keep ahead" in school. When you are having a hard time in school, you can keep ahead in your feelings about yourself, in your desire to overcome your difficulties, and in the activities in your life that you are very good at. Everyone can and should keep ahead in some ways. Many students have to work especially hard to keep ahead in their feelings about themselves. This is because their performance in school is so disappointing to their parents, their teachers, and themselves. Very often these students have various kinds of learning disorders.

HOW LEARNING DISORDERS AFFECT YOUR LIFE

Learning disorders are problems that affect some students. These problems make it hard to keep up in school. This doesn't mean that students with learning disorders are dumb. Their problems are not their fault. In fact, a student can be born with a learning disorder, but no one will know about it until the student tries to do certain things in school. For example, it is possible to be born with a weakness in your memory that doesn't cause any trouble until you try to learn the multiplication tables or write a book report. Learning disorders can affect just about everything you try to do in school and also many things you try to do outside school.

Kinds of Learning Disorders

There are many different kinds of learning disorders, and some of them cause big problems for kids. Learning disorders may make it hard for someone to learn to read, write, spell, or do mathematics. As we shall see, there are also learning disorders that wreck your ability to make friends and be popular with other kids. A learning disorder may make it hard for you to concentrate; it may cause your mind to drift or wander a lot of the time. A learning disorder can affect your memory or your ability to understand and use language as well as other students in your class. One form of learning disorder can ruin the way your brain figures out certain kinds of information coming in through your eyes. Another kind of learning disorder makes it hard to solve problems and think about certain types of ideas. Some learning disorders affect the way your muscles work. Somehow, your brain may not tell your fingers or your arms and legs exactly what to do and when to do it. Poor messages from your brain to your muscles can make you hate writing or have trouble playing certain sports. Most kids who have school problems have more than one kind of learning disorder. For this reason, we will talk about a kid's learning disorders instead of his or her learning disorder.

The Positive and Negative Sides of Learning Disorders

A learning disorder is not a disease. When you have a disease or an illness, it usually has a definite cause. The disease is abnormal, and we hope it can be cured. A disease like chicken pox has no good parts to it. But learning disorders are not completely bad for you. In fact, sometimes, having learning disorders can help you develop your strengths. For example, dealing with learning disorders can teach you how to bounce back from feeling low, how to solve problems, how to come from behind and end up a winner. Some students who have nothing but success all through school never really learn how to deal with problems. Such students may not be ready for the real world when they grow up and have problems at work or at home. So, there really is a bright side to learning disorders!

Unfortunately, though, certain learning disorders can make school very rough for you at a time when you'd like to be admired and in a place where you should be feeling successful. Also, if you can't learn and work very well in school, you may have a hard time becoming the kind of adult that you would like to become. So, if school is a problem for you because you have learning disorders, you need to understand them and try to overcome them so that they won't stop you from having success when you grow up.

The Causes of Learning Disorders

Sometimes learning disorders seem to run in families. Brothers and sisters, cousins, parents and their children may be similar in their learning disorders. You may have trouble reading, and you may find that your mother or father or uncle had the same kind of problem in elementary school. Sometimes an illness that you have early in life may bring on a learning disorder later, but proving this kind of connection can be pretty difficult. Actually, we don't really know what causes most learning disorders. We do know that they usually have something to do with differences in the ways people's brains work.

HOW THE BRAIN AFFECTS ABILITIES

In most cases, a student with learning disorders has part of his or her brain that does not work well when it has to do certain things. In fact, though, nobody's brain is perfect. Some people can't learn to whistle. Others have trouble remembering names. Some people can never learn to play the piano, juggle, sing, or recall telephone numbers. Because everyone has different strengths and weaknesses, we are all different from each other in the ways in which we function. That's why kids with learning disorders are really not so different from everybody else. But, unfortunately, kids with learning disorders have differences that interfere with their academic lives. For example, if you're not so good at juggling, you can still do well in school. However, if you are not so good at remembering what certain words look like, school can become a big problem for you. Fortunately, we can work on learning disorders even when we don't know what caused them. Of course, we do need to figure out what *kinds* of learning disorders are causing a student to have trouble when he or she is trying to succeed in school. Since most learning disorders have something to do with the way our brains operate, it is probably a good idea to present some facts about the human brain and how it is supposed to work.

The Central Nervous System

As you may know, your brain and your spinal cord, which runs down your back, make up your central nervous system. It is called *central* because it serves as the central "office" for all kinds of information and jobs.

The Spinal Cord: The central nervous system is divided into regions, each with its own jobs to accomplish. The region at the bottom is the spinal cord inside the middle of your back. The spinal cord receives all the information from nerves in your skin and muscles—information about things like temperature, pain, and your position in space. The spinal cord is also responsible for sending out orders through nerves that connect with muscles so the muscles can move the right way when you want them to. This information that keeps coming into and going out of the spinal cord connects the higher parts of the brain to various parts of your body. (You can see an illustration of the higher parts of the brain on page 7.)

The Brain: Your brain, located inside your skull, is made up of billions of tiny nerve fibers that connect with each other in many different ways. The brain is so complicated in its "wiring" that it should not be surprising that no two brains are exactly the same. This means that there can be a great number of different learning strengths and learning disorders among people, including kids in school. Sometimes it's hard to be sure what's normal and what's abnormal.

The Brainstem: The brainstem is just above the spinal cord. It gets information and sends out signals to the skin and muscles of your head and neck. The brainstem also works like an extension cord for some of your senses, including hearing and touching. For example, if you touch something with your left thumb, the feeling that you get has to pass through nerves that go through the brainstem to get to parts of your brain that can think about what you've touched. Incidentally, smelling and hearing do not have to go through the brainstem. They are allowed to connect directly with the thinking parts of the brain (without an "extension cord").

Your brainstem also has other responsibilities. It controls swallowing, breathing, talking, heart rate, the flow of your blood and your ability to see. By the way, the brainstem does not have only pleasant chores; it's the part of the brain that makes you vomit!

The Cerebellum: In the back of your brain is a region called the cerebellum. The cerebellum is responsible for fine tuning your muscle movements. It is the cerebellum that can make you really excellent at doing things with your hands or at playing a sport.

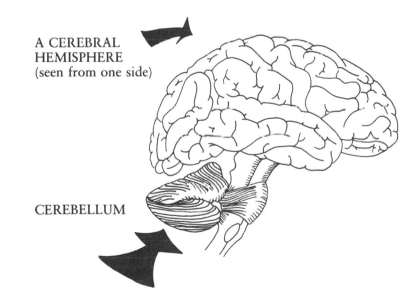

A CEREBRAL
HEMISPHERE
(seen from one side)

CEREBELLUM

The diagram above shows two important parts of the brain: one of the cerebral hemispheres and the cerebellum. The hemispheres are parts of the brain where a lot of important thinking and feeling goes on. The cerebellum is important for helping create smooth muscular movements.

A great football player, artist, or guitarist must have a super cerebellum! The cerebellum almost never gets any credit for its work. It may be that a great athlete should receive a trophy for having the "cerebellum of the year." The cerebellum works very closely with the *basal ganglia*. The basal ganglia are groups of nerves that cooperate with the cerebellum to make muscles work very smoothly so that they don't shake too much or keep missing the mark when they try to do something.

The Hypothalamus and the Thalamus: Up above the brainstem are two important parts of the brain called the hypothalamus and the thalamus. The hypothalamus performs many crucial functions. It helps control your appetite, your thirst, and the temperature of your body. The hypothalamus also has a lot to do with certain feelings that you get. For example, the hypothalamus helps you deal with both angry and peaceful feelings. The thalamus, which is right above the hypothalamus, is like a great relay station. It receives all the signals from lower parts of the body, such as your arms and legs, and sends them up to the higher regions of your brain. Every sense except smell goes up through the thalamus. You can also say that the thalamus is like a fuse box. Just as electricity comes into your home through the fuse box and then gets sent on to various rooms, information from your senses goes through the thalamus on its way to the regions of the brain that will think about it and use it.

The Cerebral Hemispheres: The highest region of your brain is divided into two halves that are joined together by millions of nerve fibers. These two halves are called the cerebral hemispheres. The two hemispheres look alike. But if you study them carefully under a microscope there are differences between them. In most

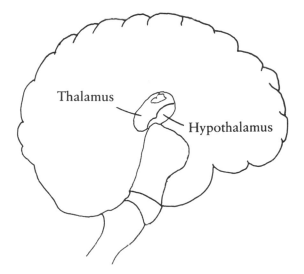

In this illustration, you can see that the hypothalamus and the thalamus are located deep within the brain. The hypothalamus controls many basic body functions, including appetite, thirst, and body temperature. The thalamus is an important relay station for messages or sensations coming up through the spinal cord and heading for the cerebral hemispheres.

people, the *left hemisphere* controls language and information that comes in or goes out in a particular sequence or order. The *right hemisphere* often specializes in visual patterns and in information, like the parts of someone's face, that comes in all at once. The left hemisphere often likes to work more quickly, while the right hemisphere is a bit slower.

The Lobes of the Brain: To complicate things, each of the hemispheres is divided into lobes. The *frontal lobes* are right behind your forehead. In some ways they are the "orchestra

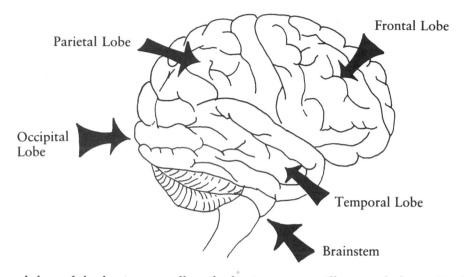

Four lobes of the brain, as well as the brainstem, are illustrated above. Each of these has very specific functions. For example, the occipital lobe plays a big role in vision, and the temporal lobe helps a person understand language.

leaders" of the brain. They help you to concentrate by allowing you to find and use the proper part of the brain for whatever you're doing at the moment. Your frontal lobes will "light up" the part of your brain that figures out language when someone is talking to you. At the same time, your frontal lobes might turn down the visual parts of your brain so you won't be too distracted while you're listening. The frontal lobes also help you control your behavior and your emotions. Therefore, they can help you get along with other people. A lot of popular kids have outstanding frontal lobes!

Behind the frontal lobes are the *parietal lobes*. The parietal lobes contain the *sensory cortex* which is the part of the brain that receives information from all of your sensory organs such as your eyes, your ears, your skin, and your sense of smell. The sensory cortex helps you figure out what these different sensations mean and what to do about them. Once you have decided what to do about your sensations, you can tell your muscles to work in a particular way. Getting muscles to move takes place at the back of each frontal lobe just in front of the parietal lobe in the *motor cortex*. Each motor cortex may seem a bit mixed up because the motor cortex in the right hemisphere controls all the muscles on the left side of your body, and the motor cortex in the left hemisphere moves all the muscles on the right side of your body. The motor cortex works closely with the cerebellum and basal ganglia so that your muscle movements will be smooth and accurate.

The *occipital lobes* sit just behind the parietal lobes. The occipital lobes help you understand information that comes in through your eyes. They figure out what you're seeing so that you can tell whether something is on top of, underneath, or next to something else. The occipital lobes help you catch a ball and do other complicated things with your eyes.

The *temporal lobes* are just beneath the parietal lobes. They have a lot to do with information such as language that comes in through your ears. Your temporal lobes are also needed for memory. But memory is scattered everywhere throughout the brain, and there are many different kinds of memory. For example, there is memory for faces, vocabulary words, spelling, and smells.

Since nobody completely understands all parts of the brain and their connections, nobody completely understands all the possible disorders that can cause kids to have a very hard time at school. Fortunately, there are many important things we do know. This book is intended to help students understand what

What you have just read in the preceding paragraphs is actually a very quick "tour" of the brain. As we have said, the brain is extremely complicated. Different regions of the central nervous system have to work very hard during a school day. Parts of the central nervous system are connected with each other, and they have to communicate with little time off. There are still many brain parts and activities that nobody understands. Experts spend their whole lives studying the human brain, but we still don't know exactly how people think or how they remember.

we know about learning disorders. If a student has learning disorders and understands what they are and how they work, life will be a lot easier.

HOW LEARNING DISORDERS CAN CREATE MISUNDERSTANDINGS

One of the big problems with learning disorders is that they can cause kids to be misunderstood by grown-ups. Also, a kid with learning disorders might not understand himself or herself. Learning disorders may look just like laziness, when really the problem isn't laziness at all. A student may appear to be lazy because she is not getting good results in school, and then she just stops trying. For some students, schoolwork requires superhuman effort, so much effort that they may decide not to try.

This can make people think that they are poorly motivated or that they just don't care (when they really do care a lot).

WHY SOME KIDS WITH LEARNING DISORDERS PUT ON DISGUISES

Learning disorders can make a kid look or feel dumb or stupid. Sometimes when students feel dumb, they intentionally put on some disguises, hoping no one will find out that they feel dumb. These disguises might include being very cool, becoming a class clown, acting tough and getting into fights, pretending not to care about school, criticizing school (saying it's useless or dumb) or becoming very quiet in order not to be noticed.

Unfortunately, a disguise may cause more problems than a learning disorder itself! Sometimes parents or teachers notice behavior that is really a disguise, and they think that the behavior itself is the whole problem. A teacher might say: "If only you would behave, you'd start doing better in school." Down deep inside yourself, you might think: "If only I could do better in school, I might start behaving. If I got good grades, I wouldn't need to act so tough and cool."

The disguises that cause the most trouble are found among students who do not understand their own learning disorders. Misunderstandings can lead to nasty arguments. Once you understand your learning disorders, as well as your strengths, there is a whole lot you can do about them, so you may not need to disguise them as much. You can actually work on them and around them!

"School is dumb. . . . I'm not gonna use any of that stuff when I grow up and become a professional skateboarder."

Some kids try to put down school. They criticize it. They say it's useless. Often, they say these things because they feel bad about how they are doing in school. In other words, they are trying to cover up their true feelings or fears about schoolwork.

HOW THIS BOOK CAN HELP YOU

This book is not supposed to help you diagnose yourself or figure out exactly what's right and what's wrong in your brain. That's very hard to do. There are experts who are trained to give tests and study your schoolwork to find out which learning disorders are a problem for you. This book should help you understand many different kinds of learning disorders; you might

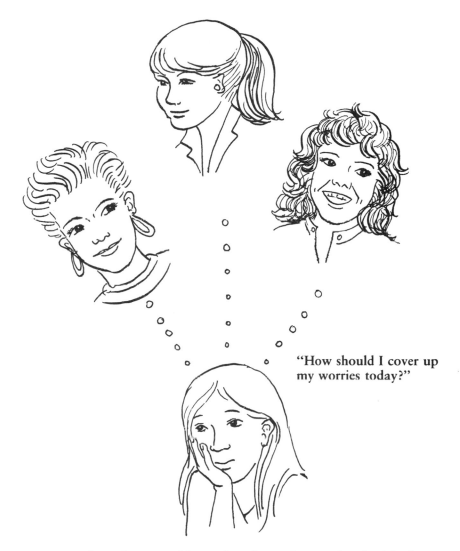

"How should I cover up my worries today?"

Many students have problems that they take to school with them. They often feel it is important to cover up their problems, to appear happy when they are really worried. To do this, they "put on" disguises to make other people think that they have no problems. Inside, however, such kids may be very anxious.

wonder about the presence of some of these in yourself or in your best friend! If there are parts of yourself that you recognize in this book, you can mention them to your parents, teachers, or other adults who are trying to help and understand you. For example, you might say to a school psychologist, "I think I might have a language disorder. From your tests, do you think this is possible?" In other words, this book may help you to help other people think about you. In a way, you can become a member of a team that is trying to understand and improve your life at school. Your ideas and your opinions are very important and often correct. You should not be afraid to speak up about yourself and what you think you need. More than anything else, this book is intended to help you feel good about school, about yourself, and about the things that make you different from everyone else.

A Way To Read Each Chapter

Each of the upcoming chapters in this book will begin with a story about a student who has one or several kinds of learning disorders discussed in the chapter. As you read these descriptions, or stories, notice not only the learning disorders but also the strengths that each of these kids has. Following the story, there will be questions for you to think about or discuss after you have read the chapter.

CHAPTER TWO

Attention—Keeping the Mind and Body in Control

STAN'S STORY

Stan is a mystery to everyone. He seems to be so smart. He's full of good ideas. He has a great sense of humor and a fantastic imagination. On some days he does well in school: he hands in his homework and gets good grades on tests. On other days he just can't seem to do anything right. Nobody understands why. Stan's parents and teachers keep telling him that they know he's smart, that they know he can really do the work when he tries to. Stan thinks he's trying, but sometimes trying is not so easy.

When Stan tries to sit and listen in class, his mind seems to drift away, and he feels a little tired. He often gets restless when he has to sit still, and he keeps thinking about the future—about what's coming next, about what he's going to do after school, about what plans he can think up for the weekend.

Stan also daydreams a lot. Last week the teacher said something about the sky being cloudy. Stan started to think about the sky. That made him think about flying and about airplanes. Then he began to think about flying at the speed of light—in a jet that's powered by making its own lightning. That made him wonder about what it would be like to be launched in a satellite. He thought it would be neat to be an astronaut someday. He began to think about being the first astronaut on Mars, and that made him wonder about whether there is any life on Mars. Next, he was imagining the fun it would be to be one of the first earth people to make friends with a Mars person.

Within two minutes, Stan was becoming popular on Mars while the teacher was explaining some word problems from yesterday's math assignment. Stan completely missed what she was saying because he was socializing in outer space. Stan's daydreams are very interesting and creative (even more fascinating than word problems). If he could ever write them down on paper, they would make super stories. But his active imagination often makes him miss out on important things going on in real life.

Stan's teachers have noticed that when he does his work, he does it too quickly. He rushes through tests and makes a lot of careless mistakes. He hates to check over his work; he says that's boring. In fact, Stan gets bored easily in school, and when he gets bored, it's hard for him to concentrate. When he's having trouble concentrating, he gets even more bored. He can concentrate well only when the ideas or activities are very, very interesting to him.

Behavior in school is sometimes a problem for Stan, too. He doesn't mean to cause trouble, but he does so many things so quickly and without thinking that he gets himself into trouble. He might talk out in class and say something that annoys the teacher, or he might do something that annoys the kid next to him. It all happens so fast that he seems to have very little control over what he is saying or doing.

Stan worries about himself. He can't understand why he has so many good ideas but still has trouble doing well in school. Stan makes himself nervous because he never knows what he will do next, what will cause him to get into trouble again, or how hard it will be for him to concentrate. He knows he has many strengths. He notices things no one else does. He thinks up great inventions and ideas. But when it comes to all the little details in school and boring responsibilities at home, he just keeps on failing. That makes him nervous, too. When he sees all the other kids concentrating, controlling their behavior, and working well, he starts to wonder whether he's just plain dumb, a little bit crazy, or just a "loser." Despite all this, many people who know Stan believe that he has a great mind and that someday he'll be a winner.

Thinking More about Stan

Try answering the following questions about Stan after reading all of Chapter 2.

- What kind of learning disorder causes the most trouble for Stan?
- What should Stan know in order to feel better about himself?
- How can Stan help himself or get help from others?

THE IMPORTANCE OF ATTENTION

Paying attention is sometimes called concentrating. In this chapter we will use both terms *attention* and *concentration*, since they mean about the same thing. The ability to concentrate or control your attention is needed to do well in school, although just about everybody has some trouble with attention sometimes. Most of us have been warned: "Pay attention," "Watch what you're doing," or "Keep your mind on your work." Yet, as we will see, concentrating is not always easy. Attention is a complicated function. For some students it's especially hard because their minds get out of control. They find that they keep "tuning in" and "tuning out" as their minds wander or drift off in a classroom. They may not listen well or hear what the teacher is saying, and this causes problems for them. To understand attention and problems with it, it is important to understand how attention gets controlled by our brains.

HOW ATTENTION IS CONTROLLED

Deciding What To Concentrate On

In school there is so much to watch, to listen to, and to think about. When you sit in a classroom, you can watch the teacher, the other students, the chalkboard, the bulletin board, or the tree outside the window. You can listen to the teacher, the clock ticking, some noise in the corridor, or the ventilation system. You can be thinking about what your teacher is saying, about what you're going to be doing after school, about the clothing that the kid next to you is wearing, or about some problems that you're having with your brother or sister.

Doing well in school is in some ways like watching television. In order to see what you want to on TV, you have to tune in the right channel at the right time. Not only that, you must concentrate on the right channel for the *right amount of time* if you want to get enough out of the program. In school, at-

Attention—the Brain's Channel Selector: *This boy is staying tuned in to the right channel; he is tuned in to what his teacher is saying. He has not turned on any of the other channels that he could be paying attention to in the classroom. At least for now, he has good selective attention.*

tention is your brain's channel selector when you are trying to decide what to watch, to listen to, to think about, or to ignore.

Filtering Out Distractions

Let's continue with the comparison of doing well in school and watching TV. To pay attention to TV, you have to keep your eyes on the screen. In school, if your attention is going to work right, it must filter out all kinds of noise and distraction. Many machines have filters in them. Air conditioners contain filters to remove dust from the air. There are filters in a car that keep the gasoline and oil clean. Chemists use filters to purify chemicals. People use filters to make coffee. That way they can drink a pure liquid without having to taste the coffee grounds. You can think about your brain in the same way. You can imagine that your brain also has filters to help you clean out distractions. Distractions are sounds, sights, or ideas that are unimportant or have nothing to do with the important thing going on at the moment.

Here are some of the distractions you have to filter out.

1. **Unimportant things you can see.** There is no use in looking out the window when you're supposed to be reading.

2. **Unimportant sounds you can hear.** It's a waste of time to listen to an air conditioner when a teacher is explaining your homework assignment to you.

3. **Your body.** You can't keep thinking about how you look, about how you feel, or about little body sensations such as the itchy feeling of a wool sweater against the back of your neck.

4. **Daydreams.** You can miss a lot if your imagination carries you away from reality. Somehow, you have to be able to filter out your daydreams most of the time in school, even though you think up some good ideas and exciting possibilities while you're daydreaming.

5. **Thoughts about the future.** If you should be concentrating on the present, you can't be thinking about the coming afternoon or night or weekend. To pay attention to the present, you have to filter out the future (at least for the moment).

6. **Things you want.** We all have needs and wants. Some of them have no connection with what we're doing at the moment. Concentrating too much or too often on such wants makes it hard to focus on anything else. If you keep thinking about chocolate or about a new game or some clothes you'd like to buy, you will find it hard to stay tuned in when there are important ideas to understand in class.

7. **Other kids.** Fellow students are sometimes the hardest things to filter out! In a classroom, they surround you. It's almost impossible to ignore them completely. But, for at least some of the time, you need to filter them out so that you can read a book, listen to the teacher, or think about your work.

You don't need to filter out *all* of these seven kinds of distractions *all* of the time. You need to pay some attention at certain times to friends, to the future, to the things you want, to sights, to sounds, to your body, and to your original ideas. There are even times when it's good to daydream. You can come up with some excellent ideas when you let your mind wander off. There are also times when it's good to gaze all around you at interesting things. A lot of artists are good at

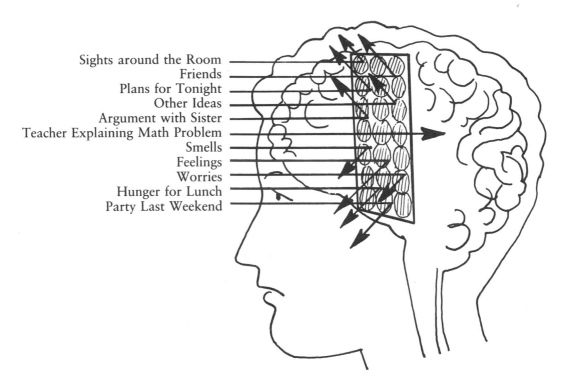

Sights around the Room
Friends
Plans for Tonight
Other Ideas
Argument with Sister
Teacher Explaining Math Problem
Smells
Feelings
Worries
Hunger for Lunch
Party Last Weekend

It is possible to imagine that our brains have filters in them. We might call these "distraction filters" because they filter out unnecessary interference when we are trying to concentrate. In this picture, you can see some of the kinds of interference that need to get filtered out by your brain so that you can concentrate well. Sounds, the future, friends, sights, and things you want may need to be filtered out while you are trying to do or think about something else.

noticing things other people miss. It's really a matter of how you divide up your attention and *when* you concentrate on *what*. When your attention is working properly, your "filters" are adjusted just right. They know exactly how much distraction to let in.

So, we have talked about two important controls over attention: choosing the most important thing to concentrate on and filtering out the unimportant things. These controls affect information coming into the brain. But there is another kind of concentration that is just as important; it is called reflecting or planning.

Reflecting or Planning

When you reflect or plan, you concentrate on things before you ever say or do them. By planning things, your brain predicts what you will do and how it will sound or look. If, during the time you are planning, it looks as if the results will be bad, you can think of some other way to do what you need to do. In fact, you can keep thinking up different ways of doing something until you come up with the best way. Planning takes time. When you're in a hurry, you can be impulsive.

An *impulse* is a feeling that you get that makes you do something very quickly without thinking or planning. You might have the impulse to say something mean or to take something away from someone or to guess at a question on a test. If you are impulsive, you sometimes act too quickly, and often you don't take the time to notice how things are going. By slowing down and concentrating *before* doing something, it is possible to control impulses so that you get better results. You can see that control over impulses is needed for good behavior and for good learning.

Concentrating While Doing Something

It is also important to be able to concentrate *while* you are doing something. By concentrating at that point, you can control what's happening. You are much more likely to get the right answer or do the best job when you're watching what you're doing. Unfortunately, concentrating while you're working also takes time. If you don't concentrate, you can work much faster. But then the results are often terrible, loaded with careless mistakes. So, you can see that working at the right speed—not too fast and not too slowly—plays a big part in attention. It takes time to concentrate, and it takes concentration to do things at the right speed!

Self-monitoring

You even need to go back and concentrate on what you've finished. This is called self-monitoring, and it can be one of the hardest jobs of all. A monitor is someone who makes sure things are done right and who reports back when something or someone has gone wrong. In the same way, there are "monitors" in your brain that check on what you've done so you can make corrections or changes if they are necessary. When you take a spelling test, for example, a monitor inside you might go back over the words to make sure that they look right before you hand them in. When you do a math assignment, your brain acts as a monitor when you check over the problems to make sure they're accurate. After writing a book report, the monitor helps you look it over to find any mistakes in spelling, punctuation, or capitalization.

So, we can see that you have to have good attention before you start something, while you're doing it, and even after you've finished.

Self-monitoring: *This girl is not only working; she is also watching herself working and thinking about her thinking to make sure that she is doing a good job. This is called self-monitoring. It is as if there is an observer inside her head to find her mistakes while she does things like math problems.*

So far we've discussed five important things about attention:

1. Choosing the right "channel" to focus on at the right time and for the right amount of time.

2. Filtering distractions

3. Planning things and controlling impulses

4. Regulating speed

5. Self-monitoring

Being Alert

In order for your attention to work well, you have to be alert and wide awake. When you're tired, it's really hard to concentrate. When you're sleeping, it's impossible to concentrate (except on your dreams)! There are parts of your brain that actually control how awake you are. There are bundles of nerves (in the brainstem) which turn down your concentration at night so you can fall asleep and then turn it up in the morning so you can be tuned in and alert all day. If your attention is not completely turned on, you become tired in the classroom. When you're tired, you become fidgety, and you're much more likely to tune out. Alertness is critical for attention.

Imagine a soldier whose job it is to stand guard at night. In order for him to detect an enemy, he must be fully alert and awake throughout the time he's on guard duty. The more tired he becomes, the less he pays attention and the more chance he has of missing important details, such as the approach of an airplane or ship. In the same way, in a classroom, the more your brain feels tired, the less you can concentrate on important details. Sleeping soundly the night before can help a student be more alert and tuned in during class the next day. When a kid feels too tired in class, she or he must try hard to stay alert. Sometimes writing things down or repeating what the teacher is saying under your breath can help you stay alert.

Controlling Your Moods

Another part of attention has to do with your moods. How you feel influences how well you concentrate. If you are unhappy or depressed about something, it can be almost impossible to concentrate in school. When your moods or feelings bounce around too much, when you keep going from very happy to very sad, it's hard to pay attention. Because of this, control over moods is needed for attention.

Controlling Your Body

Finally, you need to control the movement of your body. If you're on the go all the time, if you can't slow down, how can you concentrate? You know what it's like to take a picture when you keep moving the camera. The picture comes out too blurry. Even a movie or video camera has to move at the right speed if the tape or film is to come out looking sharp. Our bodies and minds need to work together. It's tough when you have a mind that works slowly and a body that goes too fast! You need physical activity control.

At this point, you understand something about how attention

Now, let's summarize all the different things that affect attention—things that control it.

1. Choosing the right "channel" to concentrate on at the right time and for the right amount of time

2. Filtering distractions

3. Planning things and controlling impulses

4. Regulating speed

5. Self-monitoring

6. Staying alert and awake

7. Controlling moods

8. Controlling activity

works, so let's take a look at what it's like to have problems with attention. Such problems are called attention deficits.

ATTENTION DEFICITS

The word *deficit* in this part of this book is important. If you borrow money to buy more things than your allowance can pay for, you are said to have a "budget deficit." That means that either you need a bigger allowance, or you need to spend less money. In the same way, someone with an attention deficit needs to pay more attention than he or she seems able to. Either this person needs to find a way to have better concentration, or he or she needs to think about things that require less attention. Unfortunately, schoolwork requires a lot of attention. So, students who can't pay enough attention are likely to be thinking about the wrong things during the school day. They have problems with learning and with getting work done in school. Sometimes they also have behavior problems that get them into trouble. Yet, it's not really their fault. They have trouble with the eight controls we have just listed. Most of the time they would like to do better in school, but when they try to concentrate, it all seems too hard.

What It's Like To Have an Attention Deficit

Let's look at what makes life so hard for kids with attention deficits.

First of all, they all have serious trouble concentrating. It's hard for them to find the right channels to tune into. Also, their distraction filters don't work very well! When a student needs to be listening to a teacher, he or she might be staring out the window, thinking about plans for the weekend, or dreaming of buying a fantastic new bicycle. Such a student is "distractible." His or her filters aren't working the way they should.

Most kids with attention deficits don't like a lot of details. They get bored when there's too much information to concentrate

* Throughout this book, you will notice that geese are used periodically to point to items in a list. Why geese? The geese are used because the author raises geese on his farm and observes that they are very good at making discoveries when they stick their necks out. Geese are often used as artwork in the author's publications.

on. But as you go through school, there are more and more little details to concentrate on, and there are more distractions too. So, concentration is a real challenge.

Kids with attention deficits may hand in work that is embarrassing to them and confusing to the teacher. The work might be messy, or it might have ideas in it that are not as good as the ideas in their heads.

Many kids with attention deficits are impulsive. They do things much too quickly and without planning and organizing. They have trouble slowing down and concentrating when they work, so they make too many careless mistakes. Also, they don't do self-monitoring. Remember, self-monitoring means looking over what's been done to make sure there aren't any silly mistakes.

While some students with attention deficits are impulsive when it comes to schoolwork, others are impulsive in their behavior. (Some are impulsive in their behavior *and* their schoolwork.) In terms of behavior, an impulsive person might get very angry and then all of a sudden hit someone. She wouldn't really mean to do it. It would just happen so fast that there would be no time to think about what she was doing and to come up with some other ways of handling the situation. Some impulsive students get into trouble because they do things they don't really mean to do. It's just too hard for them to stop and think before they act. If they could slow down before acting, they probably would not get into as much trouble. Unfortunately, sometimes the grown-ups in their lives don't understand. They often think that an impulsive kid is really mean or bad for doing a particular thing. The adults don't realize that the kid really didn't have full control at the moment. For students with attention deficits, things often happen too fast!

Some students with attention deficits have a lot of trouble waking up in the morning to go to school, and some have trouble falling asleep at night. They stay up very late. Some kids say they can concentrate much better at night than they can during the day. Anyway, there are some students with attention deficits who have a hard time keeping alert in school. They get very tired when they try to concentrate. Sometimes they feel as if they're going to fall asleep in class. Other times they just feel like yawning and stretching. Many of them find that they have to move around a lot in order to stay fully awake and tuned in. They also find that when they try to concentrate for a long time, they get bored and tired. That means that there are many things they start but don't finish. Finishing can be a big problem for them. It just makes them tired to work on something or think about something for a long time. Some people say that these kids have a short *attention span.* What these people mean is that kids with attention deficits don't concentrate *long enough*.

Many people with attention deficits have trouble controlling their desires for the things they want. They seem to want things all the time, and as soon as they get the things they want, they don't want them as much anymore. Instead, they want something else. In other words, they are too hard to satisfy! When they want something, they want it badly, and they just can't wait; they have to have it right away. They "bug" their parents until they get it. Sometimes they can really wear out their parents by asking for things all the time. It can also bother their brothers and sisters who think it's not fair that the kid with attention deficits wants and gets things all the time. This can lead to some big arguments in the family.

 Some kids with attention deficits have trouble controlling their moods. They seem to vary too much from being very happy to being very sad. They never feel quite right, and it's hard to predict how they are going to feel from one moment to the next.

There are kids with attention deficits who are hyperactive. They move all the time. You may know someone in school who is called "hyper." This is usually a kid who is on the go all the time; he or she just can't slow down. Someone who is hyperactive may have trouble sitting still; or he or she may actually get very tired and have to move around in order to feel good and stay alert. Many kids who are hyperactive like to drive very fast on their bicycles. Some love skateboards, motorcycles, and fast-moving cars. They like to be outdoors a lot and to keep in motion as much as possible. They have tremendous energy; they keep their motors running all the time! But not everyone with attention deficits is hyperactive. Some kids have very active minds but are able to control their bodies so that they are regular in their activity. Still others are even *inactive*.

Kids with attention deficits do not have problems with attention *all of the time.* Instead, as we said earlier, they seem to tune in and tune out. Their attention is strong sometimes, but it is also often weak. This means that they are inconsistent. They concentrate sometimes, and then they lose their concentration at other times. The fact that they are so inconsistent can be very confusing to everyone. A student with attention deficits may have a very good morning in school and then do poorly that afternoon. He or she may do well one day and have great trouble concentrating the next day. In high school, a student with attention deficits may have grades that keep rising and falling like a bouncing ball. Quiz scores may go from a 96 to a 44, then to a 90, and then to a 30. Unless it is known that such a student has attention deficits, no one can figure out why the grades vary this way.

Sometimes people accuse a student of not studying hard enough or, "applying herself," when she gets a grade like a 30. But really the student might not have been concentrating correctly while studying for the test. We really don't know why kids with attention deficits are so inconsistent in school and sometimes

What Some Kids Have Said about Their Attention: The following things said by students with attention deficits can help us better understand these students.

"My head is just like a television set—except it has no channel selector. So I get all the programs on my screen at the same time."

"When I sit in class, I keep having these 'mind drifts.' I never know when my mind is gonna drift away so I lose what's happening."

"I like to move around a lot. When I sit still, I get tired. I get bored. I need action."

"I think I'm just a 'busticator'. A busticator is someone who busts things up all the time. He doesn't mean to. He's real fast and keeps getting into trouble for not

thinking. You know it's not really his fault that he does things fast, but I guess he has to take the blame when he causes trouble or bothers someone. Anyway, that's me. I'm a real busticator."

"When I sit in class, I keep thinking about things at home. I think about my dog, my sister, and my mother and my dad. I think about what we did last summer and how much fun it would be to go back to the beach again this year. I think about next weekend, and I think about what will be on television tonight. I think about everything except school!"

"I was looking at the bulletin board. I noticed that there were seven thumbtacks in the bulletin board but only six of them were being used. I wondered about the seventh thumbtack. Why was there nothing underneath it? Maybe someone had pulled something off, or maybe it had fallen off. I thought about pulling the thumbtack out of the bulletin board. I thought it might even be cool to put it on the seat of the kid in front of me. I noticed that this thumbtack was red and all the others were either blue or green. I wondered why the red thumbtack was the one with nothing under it. Maybe there was a reason for it. I tried to think of some reasons. Then, all of a sudden, the teacher called on me, and I realized I had no idea what had been going on in the classroom. The teacher was telling us important stuff while I was busy with that dumb thumbtack. That keeps on happening to me. I'm so distractible. All kinds of things pull me off track."

in their behavior. We do know that they concentrate much better on things that they really enjoy than they do on things that are not much fun. So, a kid with attention deficits may concentrate for hours on a hobby or television but then tune out when doing school work or thinking about other information that is not too exciting.

Is It Ever Good To Have Attention Deficits?

Yes, it can be good to have attention deficits! They can cause kids to do poorly in school, and they can cause behavior problems, but many kids with attention deficits have thoughts and ideas that no one else would ever think of. Not only are these kids creative, they are also smart. Many kids with attention deficits can remember little details from far in the past better than most other people. Impulsive or hyperactive people can get a lot done during one day. They are on the move all the time. Their high energy allows them to accomplish much more than other people in the same amount of time. In fact, many grown-ups with attention deficits are very successful. They include artists, actors, actresses, business people, and all kinds of other adults. This means that if you have attention deficits you should not get discouraged. It's possible to improve your ability to concentrate and actually to use the way your attention works to become a unique and exciting person.

What Causes Attention Deficits?

Most of the time we don't know why a student has attention deficits. It's likely that he or she was just born that way. Attention deficits may be inherited just like the color of one's hair. While we don't know the exact cause of attention deficits in all people, we do have some ideas about what may cause them in some people. Some students with attention problems may have a weakness in the part of the brainstem that regulates sleeping and waking. That weakness makes it hard for them to sleep well at night and then be alert in school. Others may have a minor problem in the frontal lobes (See page 9) that control some parts of behavior and concentration. Really, it doesn't matter what caused an attention deficit. What we must do is know as much as we can about it, and then we must try to keep the deficit under good control.

Keeping Attention Deficits under Control

Some things can make attention problems worse. Some children and parents have observed that when they eat certain foods, their attention gets weaker. It's as if those foods somehow clog up the mind's filters! We know that some medicines can make attention deficits worse. So, if a student has attention problems, he or she needs to notice whether a particular food or medicine makes the problems worse. It's also true that when you don't feel well, it's hard to concentrate. You know that if you go to school with a cold and a headache, it is not so easy to pay attention.

It's also true that your attention can get out of control when you're worried a lot. If life is not going well for you and you feel sad or troubled, your attention is used up by your problems. There is too little attention left over for concentrating on a teacher or a textbook. You have to work on your problems and get them better so there can be enough attention left over for use at school.

Also, it's hard to concentrate when you don't understand some new ideas or what you're supposed to do in class. Some students have trouble paying attention because paying attention is totally useless and frustrating. Later in this book we will talk about some of the kinds of learning problems that might make it hard to understand what you're reading, what a teacher is saying, or how you're supposed to solve a problem. When a student struggles and just can't understand or do something, it's not unusual for him or her to tune out or get distracted. If your attention is weak to begin with, *and* if you do not understand very well, then you have two reasons for not concentrating.

Are Attention Deficits Common?

Yes, attention deficits are very common. They are probably the most common reason that some very good minds do poorly in school. They are also one of the common causes of behavior problems. Of course, as we said earlier, everybody has attention deficits sometimes. Everyone's mind wanders once in a while, and everyone does impulsive things occasionally. The difference between people with attention deficits and people without them is that people with them have poor control of their attention too often. This frequent lack of control affects not only their grades in school but also their success in other parts of life. It is important to realize that kids with attention deficits are not mentally ill or dumb. They are just a little different, and parts of this difference can be good.

What Can Be Done To Help People with Attention Deficits?

There is a lot that can be done to help a student overcome attentional problems. We probably can't completely "cure" attention deficits, but we should not want to change anybody completely anyway. If we can help a student with attention deficits, he or she may have fewer problems in school, at home, and with friends. Well, how do we do it? The following material will give you some ideas.

Use Pictures To Explain Problems: First, we must tell kids with attention deficits what we know about attention deficits. In fact, this book has been written to help such students understand more about themselves and what they need to work on to improve. One way that we help students understand their attention deficits is by showing them pictures that will explain their problems to them. On page 41 you can see what we call the Concentration Cockpit. This can be used to help someone understand his or her attention deficits.

To understand how the Concentration Cockpit can help you understand your attention deficits, pretend you are the pilot of an airplane. The plane itself is like your brain. It is complicated and it is able to fly fast and far. However, in order to use all of the engines well, the airplane (like your brain) needs to be controlled by a skilled pilot in the cockpit.

If you look at the drawing of the cockpit, you will see that there are many different meters and dials that are like the controls of the brain. If you read about each one, it will sound familiar because it has to do with the different parts of attention

MOOD CONTROL:
Not Getting Much Too
Sad or Much Too
Happy at the Wrong
Times

The Concentration Cockpit*

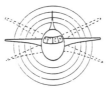

SENSORY
FILTRATION
CONTROL: Not
Paying Attention to
Unimportant Sounds
and Sights

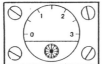

MOTOR/VERBAL
CONTROL: Not
Wasting Movement
and Talking

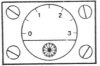

SOCIAL CONTROL:
Tuning Out Other Kids
When You Need To

APPETITE CONTROL:
Not Always Wanting
Things and Looking
Ahead

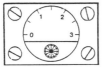

BEHAVIORAL
CONTROL: Thinking
Before You Do Things

FREE FLIGHT
CONTROL: Not
Daydreaming

MEMORY CONTROL:
Remembering Important
Things

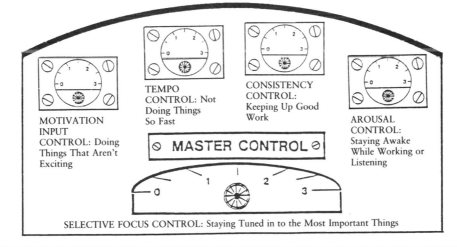

MOTIVATION
INPUT
CONTROL: Doing
Things That Aren't
Exciting

TEMPO
CONTROL: Not
Doing Things
So Fast

CONSISTENCY
CONTROL:
Keeping Up Good
Work

AROUSAL
CONTROL:
Staying Awake
While Working or
Listening

MASTER CONTROL

SELECTIVE FOCUS CONTROL: Staying Tuned in to the Most Important Things

See pages 40 and 42 for an explanation.

that we have already talked about. To help a student understand his attention deficits, we review each meter and ask the student to use a pencil to draw in the dial that is about right for him. A *zero* is poor control; a *one* is a control that is not so good; a *two* is good control; and a *three* is excellent control.

Get Help from Tutors and Counselors: Sometimes a student needs help with his or her attention. A tutor or counselor of some sort can work with a boy or girl to help to improve attention. The student and the person helping him or her can play various games that teach the student to think before doing things, to work slowly, and to pay attention to important details. In other words, a student can practice concentrating. Having someone to help can make it more fun and interesting.

Help Yourself: There is a lot you can do by yourself. First, you need to recognize when you are drifting off and losing your attention. When that happens, you need to try to adjust the knobs in your brain's "cockpit"! If being impulsive is your problem, then you will need practice planning and organizing before you do things and then working slowly. If it is self-monitoring, then you will need to practice proofreading and finding your own mistakes. If you have trouble sitting for a long time, you may need to take frequent breaks while you work. You can also practice sitting for longer and longer periods of time.

In class, it is a good idea to have a pencil in your hand most of the time. As you get older, you can take notes. If you are not yet able to take good notes, you can just write down a few important words as you hear them. You don't even have to spell the words correctly.

Get Help from Your Teacher:　It is important to try to sit as close to the teacher as possible. Sometimes you can work out an arrangement, so that the teacher signals you when you are tuned out. He or she should let you know this without the other students knowing about it. For example, the teacher might touch your shoulder when you are tuned out. It is also important for the teacher to tell you each day how your attention has been going.

Do Homework:　Doing homework can be tough. Many students find that it is best for them not to work in their bedrooms. This is where they sleep, and when doing schoolwork they should try to stay as awake as possible. Some students like to work on the floor of a living room, in the kitchen, or somewhere else. Sometimes kids will actually set up an office somewhere for working. Still others like to move around while they work. They like to use several different rooms or places to get work done. They need to take frequent breaks. Some students find that they have to listen to music while they study. This, too, is okay—if it works. Music can be an extra filter to block out other distractions. But if listening to music makes concentration worse, it shouldn't be played.

Know the Time When You Work Best:　You need to find the best time for you to concentrate. Some students are most able to concentrate right after school. Others can think better in the evenings or early in the morning. You should set up a time that best fits your own attention pattern. Then you should try to work at the same time each day—even if you don't have homework. You could be reading or writing or doing something else as an exercise to strengthen your control over attention.

Possibly Take Prescription Drugs: Some students take prescription drugs to help with their attention. These drugs are called stimulants because they help to "wake up" the person who takes them. This means that they make the person feel more alert. Several drugs are used; the most common are Ritalin, Dexedrine, and Cylert. These medicines seem to help some students with attention deficits. But they don't help everyone. Also, they don't cure; they improve the person who takes them. If you take medicine, it is important to understand that the pill isn't making you smarter, and it's definitely not a pill for crazy people. It just helps you listen better and stay more alert. The chemicals in the pills are like the chemicals that are found in coffee. Sometimes having a cup of coffee helps a grown-up concentrate better. In the same way, taking medicine for your attention may help you feel more awake and tuned in. Remember, though, that medication is not the whole story. In fact, it doesn't work at all for some students. Usually, you, your parents, and your doctor need to decide whether it would be right for you. We'll talk more about medicine in Chapter 8.

Does Good Concentration Guarantee Good Work in School?

Unfortunately, there is more to learning than attention. In the next chapter, we will talk about one very important part of school, the ability to remember things. We will see how attention and memory work closely together to help you learn well and work well.

CHAPTER THREE

Memory—Using the Brain's Storage System

MAX'S STORY

Max is a good kid whom everyone likes. In addition to having many close friends, he is popular at school and in his neighborhood. He is also a good artist who draws cartoons that are funny and realistic. In terms of his behavior, Max is no problem for his teachers or his parents.

Max does not get good grades in school, however, and it's hard to figure out why. In a class discussion, he has some of the best ideas. When you talk to him, he seems really smart. He has a good vocabulary, and he has no trouble understanding what other people are saying.

Some subjects in school are particular problems for Max. Although he understands and likes mathematics, he sometimes has trouble taking math tests because he works too slowly. He has said that he knows the multiplication tables but that it takes him a long time to remember them. While he is doing a problem, he has to think too hard and too long about things like how much 8 × 7 is. Nothing seems to flow automatically from his memory.

Max has even more difficulty with spelling and writing. When he tries to spell, he just can't picture exactly what words look like. Also, Max's handwriting is messy. He says that he has a lot of trouble remembering and writing at the same time. This is because it's very hard for him to remember how to make the letters in cursive writing at the same time that he's trying to spell correctly, punctuate, capitalize, use good vocabulary, and remember his ideas. Max once said, "Every time I try to write, I lose my memory."

Max claims that his number one problem has been copying from transparencies that the teacher puts up on a screen. Max copies too slowly. He has to keep looking up at the transparencies every few seconds because he can't remember large chunks of what's on the screen. Before he is halfway through his copying, the teacher puts a new transparency on the screen. Other kids seem to be able to look at the screen and then write a lot without having to look up again. Max's teacher sometimes criticizes him by saying that he doesn't work fast enough, that he is not really applying himself.

Max has started to hate school because he is doing so badly. Writing is so difficult for him that he avoids it whenever he can. Sometimes he doesn't even bother to hand in reports. He gets very embarrassed when other kids correct his papers and make fun of his messy writing. Max knows that he is smart. He once said, "I know I'm excellent at thinking and understanding, but there's certain stuff in school that I just can't remember well. I'd rather figure out something than have to remember it. It's especially hard for me to remember things quickly—like on a test. It's also bad when I have to remember a bunch of things all at once—like when I write."

Thinking More about Max

Try answering the following questions about Max after reading all of Chapter 3.

- What makes it so hard for Max to write?
- What are Max's strengths?
- How could Max's friends help him do better in school?

THE IMPORTANCE OF UNDERSTANDING *AND* REMEMBERING

It is possible to understand something but not remember it later. It is also possible to remember something without understanding it. But to learn, you have to understand *and* remember. Of course, it is easier to remember ideas you understand. Plus, it is much easier to understand something new when you can remember what went before it. For example, it would be hard to understand long division if you couldn't remember multiplication. So you can see that when understanding and remembering work well together, the best learning takes place. Some students who are having trouble in school understand most things pretty well, but they have trouble remembering. Others can remember better than they can understand certain kinds of facts or ideas. In this chapter, we will explore memory. In later chapters, we will talk about language, about concepts, and about figuring out things we see, all of which will help you understand understanding.

USING YOUR MEMORY

You need memory for just about everything you do in life. You remember how to brush your teeth, how to get dressed in the morning, where you left your notebook (You hope!), and what you need to do for a homework assignment. But, memory is never perfect. We all forget things. Sometimes we forget important ideas, skills, or facts. Sometimes we forget what we were supposed to do. Sometimes our memory's mistakes get us into trouble. While everyone has some problems with memory, some students have too many memory problems. It is hard for them to remember important information. They forget how to do certain things. Learning to read, solving mathematics problems, writing reports, or memorizing vocabulary words can be torture for some students with memory problems. Later in this chapter we will talk about the different jobs that memory has to do and the kinds of memory disorders that can make school frustrating for certain kids. Before we do all that, however, we must look at some facts about memory.

IMPORTANT FACTS ABOUT MEMORY

There is no one part of your brain that stores everything you know. Memory is spread out all over your brain. Facts, useful ideas, and skills are kept in many different brain locations. For example, your memory for people's faces is in one brain location, while your memory for spelling or for things that have happened to you is located in other storage places.

There is no such thing as a good or a bad memory. There are so many types of memory that when we discuss memory we must ask, "Memory for what?" Some people are very good at remembering names, while others have trouble doing this. Some people have minds like telephone books. They can remember dozens of telephone numbers, while others can hardly remember their own telephone number! So, everyone could get a memory report card with good grades in some kinds of memory and poor grades in other types of memory! No one has a memory that gets straight A's!

We have learned a lot about how memory works by studying people who have a problem called amnesia. They may get this problem from a serious head injury that makes them lose their memory. Because there are so many different kinds of memory, there are also many different kinds of amnesia. Some people lose only memory for recent events, while other people can't remember the things they learned a long time ago (like their own names or where they were born). One way that scientists have learned about memory is by studying what happens to people who have lost some of their memory.

You can store incredible quantities of information in memory. There are millions of nerves in the brain that hold a tremendous amount of information. You can store so much knowledge that some things can be hard to find when you need them. When things get "lost" in memory, it can sometimes take days to "find" or remember them.

MEMORY'S JOBS

Your memory has three basic jobs to perform. First, there is the job of *storing*. Ideas, facts, people you know, or new skills have to be stored away for future use. Second, there is the job of *finding things in memory*. You have to be able to find what you have stored. Third, there is the job of *keeping ideas together while you are working on them*. We call this *active working memory*. It is active because you are using the memory at the moment, and it is working because you are using that memory to do something. This third job of memory is important so that you don't forget what you're doing while you are doing it.

The Job of Storing

Storing in memory is very much like putting things away in different drawers. If you are careful and organized about where you put things, it will be easier to find them later. Kids who have messy rooms almost always have trouble finding the right socks or shirts. People who have very "messy" memories tend to be absentminded. They keep forgetting things because they don't know where in their minds they have stored them.

The first step in storing is understanding the sights, sounds, skills, or experiences that you might want to store. Then you have to figure out what you really need to remember. Of course, there are some things we all remember without ever deciding to remember them. For example, if someone asks you what you had for breakfast today, you might remember even though you never studied your juice, your cereal, or your toast! But a lot of memory is deliberate, and that's the kind that counts in school. Fortunately, we don't need to remember everything, even in school. When we described attention in Chapter 2, we talked about selecting important ideas to focus on and filtering out those that are unimportant. This is where attention and memory need to cooperate. People whose attentional filters are working will be better at deciding what should get stored. Kids with attention problems sometimes store too many unimportant things and throw out what they really need to remember. Sometimes they amaze people with the small details from a long time ago that they can remember. But, these same students may be failing in school because they have trouble deciding what's important to remember and what should be forgotten when they try to study.

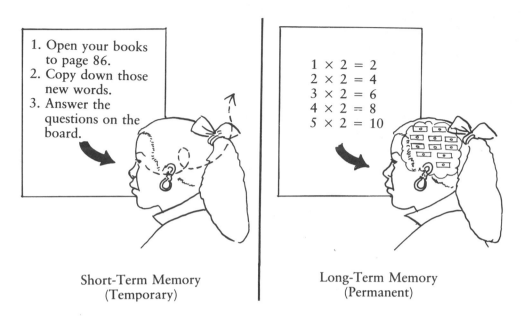

1. Open your books to page 86.
2. Copy down those new words.
3. Answer the questions on the board.

$$1 \times 2 = 2$$
$$2 \times 2 = 4$$
$$3 \times 2 = 6$$
$$4 \times 2 = 8$$
$$5 \times 2 = 10$$

Short-Term Memory
(Temporary)

Long-Term Memory
(Permanent)

In this illustration, we can see two different kinds of memory at work. On the left side is short-term memory. The girl needs to remember the instructions she is reading just long enough to complete the task. On the right side, the student is trying to remember the multiplication tables. She will need to remember them for a very long time. This information first goes into her short-term memory, and then it goes into her long-term memory storage system—her brain's "memory drawers."

Registering Things in Memory: Once you have decided what you need to store, you register the information in your memory. Registering can be compared to recording what you see or hear while it is occurring. It's like making a video tape or audio cassette.

Memory can be either short term (temporary) or long term (permanent). When you register new information, you are putting it into short-term memory. As we shall see, it can later be stored permanently if you decide that you are likely to need the information again.

Short-Term Memory: Some of the things that you "record" you will want to keep only long enough to use once. For example, if someone tells you a phone number, you may record that number in your memory, and then, once the telephone call is completed, you may erase the number from your memory. You can always look it up in a telephone directory if you need it again. Other things you may remember only long enough to figure them out. If a teacher gives you complicated instructions, you need to remember all of the directions while you're trying to understand them. But, once you know what you're supposed to do, you can just go ahead and do it, and after that you can forget the instructions. You don't want your mind cluttered up with directions for things you've already finished!

There are many examples of temporary registration in memory. During a movie, you try to remember the names of all of the characters. Remembering their names will help you understand the story. Two weeks later when you think about the movie, you probably won't remember any of the names, but you'll still remember what the movie was about. During a vacation at a hotel, you should remember your room number during your entire stay. Otherwise, you could enter the wrong hotel room and get embarrassed! A year after the vacation, it is definitely not important to remember the number of the room you stayed in, even though you will probably still remember many things that happened during that trip.

Long-Term Memory: As you have just seen, some of what we register is only temporary, but there is also a large amount of

Going through Short-Term Memory
To Get to Long-Term Memory

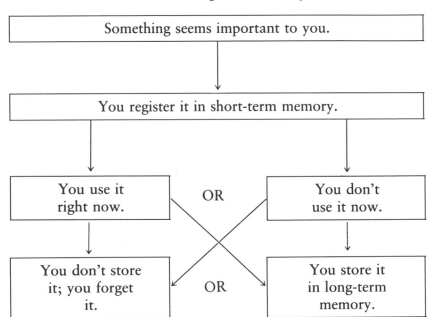

In the diagram above, you can see how information sometimes gets transferred from short-term memory to long-term memory. Several possibilities are shown: First, you realize that something seems important, so you register it in your short-term memory. Then, if you want to or need to, you can use the information right away. For example, if the information is the combination to your lock, you might use it right away to try to open the lock. Or, you might decide not to use it right away, but to transfer the information to your long-term memory so that you can find it later when you need it. It is also possible to use the information right away and then to put it into long-term memory. There is even some information that you can register and never use. This kind of information usually is pretty unimportant. For example, someone may tell you a joke. You may register that joke in short-term memory, but never tell it to anyone or even think about it again. If it is never used, it usually gets forgotten.

information and skill that is supposed to be kept permanently, that needs to get into long-term memory. For example, when you learn spelling words, important facts, or a new friend's name, you want to store these things in long-term memory. But things like that, things you deliberately store, have to pass through short-term memory and *then* get put into long-term memory (permanent storage). So, after something gets registered in short-term memory, you decide whether to forget it or to send it to long-term memory. Of course, you don't often stop and think about all this, but it happens in your mind, just the same, while you're learning.

Reconstructing Information: Although we have said that storing things in memory is like making a recording, there is one important difference. When you make a video tape, you can record a whole show and leave nothing out. When you make a "recording" in your memory, you usually can't fit everything in. Although your memory as a whole is huge, it can take in only a small amount of information at one time. This is because the short-term memory entry to that enormous long-term storage space is extremely small.

Often the information you decide to register comes in chunks that are too big to fit into short-term memory. These chunks may include some little details that are not very important anyway. For example, if you want to remember what someone looks like, you have to pick out and store the most important details of that person, such as the features that make it easy to tell him from somebody else. You must register the color of his hair, the shape of his nose, his approximate height, and several other features of his appearance. In addition, you might want to register some other things about him that will help you remember him the next time that you see him. For example, you might register the fact that he reminds you of your cousin and that he always wears nice clothes, walks slowly, and smiles at everyone.

This process of picking out important details for storage is called reconstruction. To register information, you need to reconstruct it so that it will fit into the small space of short-term memory. Think again about the example given in the last paragraph. In it, we said that to remember what a particular boy looks like, you would have to select specific details about him to store in memory. By doing this, you would "reconstruct" his image to make it compact enough to fit into short-term memory.

Another example of reconstruction might take place when you are trying to remember a story. As you listen to it, you pick out its most important parts. This is sometimes called "finding the gist of the story." You also pick out other parts that are interesting or important to you personally. For instance, there might be parts of a story that remind you of another story or of something that happened to you in your own life. These kinds of details stand out and get included in your reconstruction of the story. Different students reading the same story are likely to reconstruct the story a little differently, since each kid might find different parts of the story especially interesting or exciting to him or her.

Of course, to reconstruct a story, you must first understand it. Otherwise, it will be too hard for you to find its gist, and then you will record in memory a lot of unimportant details or story parts while you omit crucial information. Then, if you try to tell the story to someone else later, it will sound like an entirely different story. You will have constructed a new story instead of reconstructing the real story. So, understanding and remembering work together when you have to reconstruct something to register it in memory. This means that if there is something you can't remember, you should wonder whether you really understood it in the first place.

Registering Things Deeply Enough: Once you have reconstructed something so that it is meaningful and compact enough to be registered in short-term memory, there is something else that you must be concerned with. It is *depth of processing*. This has to do with how deeply you register information in memory. It is possible to think of the registration process as being similar to drawing on a piece of soft clay. If you draw very lightly, it may be hard to see the pattern you've made. It may also wear out more easily. If, on the other hand, you bear down hard, then the lines on the clay will be deep, easier to see, and harder to wear out. Another example to show differences in depths of processing is what can happen at a party. If you meet someone new and he tells you his name, you may not really listen very carefully, and then when you try to remember the name later, you'll realize that you can't. The reason that you can't recall the name is that there wasn't much depth of processing. Somehow, that name did not record strongly in your memory.

There are things you can do to increase the depth of processing. For example, you can listen very carefully when you meet someone who tells you his name. You can do this by not thinking about anything else while you are listening. Then you can whisper the name several times or picture it as if it were written on a chalkboard. All of the things we've just described are examples of memory strategies. They will impress the name deeply in your memory so that it should be easy to remember later on. We'll describe more memory strategies later in this chapter.

Your ability to reconstruct effectively and to get information registered deeply enough in short-term memory depends on a lot of things. If you are trying to remember too many things at once, registration usually isn't very good. If you are very nervous or upset about something, it is sometimes hard to register important ideas. It is as if your worries are being recorded instead of the ideas. Some kids have trouble registering information just because they are not really paying attention. When you're tuned out, there is not much depth of processing. This is one reason

Three Steps for Storing Information in Short-Term Memory

Number of Step	Name of Step	What You Have To Do
1	Deciding What To Store	• Focus your attention. • Know what's important or useful. • Filter out distractions.
2	Reconstruction	• Pick out the most important parts. • Make the information shorter— more compact. • Add any personal details that you can think of.
3	Depth of Processing	• Concentrate hard enough on what you are storing. • Use strategies. • Make sure it "gets in."

that some students with attention deficits have trouble using their memories well. The chart on page 58 summarizes storage in short-term memory. It also shows how important strong attention is for memory to work well.

Different Ways of Receiving Information

Visual Memory: There are students who can register some kinds of information but have some trouble with other kinds. For example, there are some students who find it very easy to register information in memory if that information gets to the brain through their eyes. They are excellent at reconstructing faces, streets, buildings, and places they have visited. They have a very strong visual memory.

Auditory Memory: There are others who are not so good at registering visual information. Some students are especially keen at registering what they hear. They are very good at reconstructing spoken words and sentences. It's easy for them to store spoken explanations, directions, and stories. Such students have a very good auditory memory or memory for spoken language. This helps them have a very good memory for written language (reading) too. You may find this idea confusing because although we *see* a page of writing, we remember it mostly as language.

Sequential Memory: Some information arrives at your brain arranged in a sequence or definite order. To understand it and store it well, it is important to be able to register the sequence in just the right order. As you go through school, sequences get longer and longer. Some kids have serious problems with se-

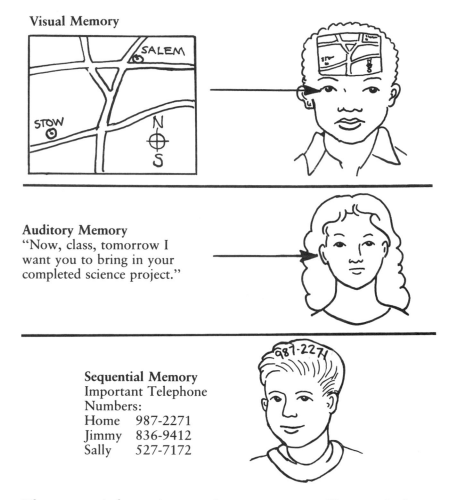

Visual Memory

Auditory Memory
"Now, class, tomorrow I want you to bring in your completed science project."

Sequential Memory
Important Telephone Numbers:
Home   987-2271
Jimmy   836-9412
Sally   527-7172

Three ways information gets into memory are illustrated above. At the top, the student is trying to store details of a map; to do so, he needs to use his visual memory. The next student is trying to register some instructions that the teacher is giving; she is using auditory or verbal memory to do so. The third kid has some very important telephone numbers he is trying to store. He has to use sequential memory, so that he can register the numbers in the right order.

quential memory. If the teacher gives them four things in a row to do, if a math problem includes five steps, or if there is a list of dates to remember in a history class, they have trouble. A lot of kids who have trouble registering sequences are confused about time (the most important sequence). Often they are late learning how to tell time. They may have trouble remembering the right order of days of the week and of months of the year. This can make them feel ignorant. We will say more about sequences in Chapter 5. Before we continue, let's do some review.

To store information in memory, our brains do the following things:

1. They try to understand the information well.

2. They decide what's most important to remember.

3. They reconstruct information so that its most important parts can be registered in memory.

4. They record information strongly—with enough depth of processing.

5. They hold the information in the right order or pattern.

Why Some Students Have Problems Registering Information: Students can have problems with registration for a lot of reasons. Some may have difficulty reconstructing information. Others may not register with enough depth of processing. Some problems with registration may be due to the fact that students don't understand, or that they can't handle the way the information comes in (visually, in language, or in a sequence). Students who have attention deficits may have trouble with memory because they choose the wrong things to store. They may hold on to some unimportant ideas for too long while losing more important information.

Long-Term Memory: We have said earlier that once new ideas, facts, or skills are registered, they can be kept in memory either for a short time or for a long time. After information has been registered and then used right away, it should be forgotten (because we no longer need it) or transferred to the long-term or permanent storage system for future use. Much of what we learn in school needs to be transferred to the long-term storage system. This system can be compared to different drawers where we can keep our knowledge or skill so that we can find it and use it when we need it. Spelling words, vocabulary, the multiplication tables, and almost everything else we learn in school should be put into the right long-term "memory drawers" so that they can be found quickly, accurately, and easily on a test or during a class discussion. As we have said, our ability to find information depends upon how organized we were when we transferred things to the drawers of long-term memory. Some students are much better at this than others.

Ways Information Gets Stored: There are four common ways that information gets stored: by pairs, by categories, by chains, or by rules.

Pairs: When we store things in pairs, we organize information so that if we see, hear, or think about one-half of a pair, we

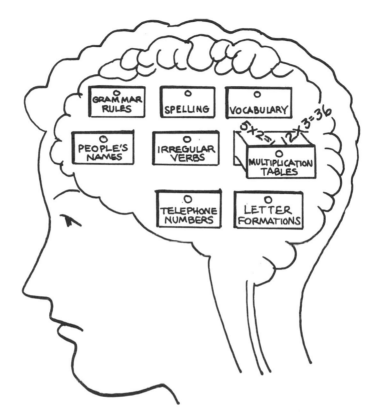

This diagram shows that in the human brain there are many different "drawers" for storing different kinds of information or skills. Different people have different-sized drawers for various kinds of information. Someone may be able to fit a tremendous amount of spelling in her spelling drawer but have trouble remembering many names because her drawer for that skill is smaller. Some kids have enough drawer space, but the drawers keep getting stuck; these kids can't get what they know out fast enough. Others can never quite find the right drawers! No one has a totally good or totally bad memory. When talking about memory, we always have to ask, "Memory for what?" or "Which drawers are easy to open and have enough room in them, and which ones don't work so well?"

will remember the other half. We store names with faces this way. If you see a girl's face, you remember her name. If you hear someone's name, you remember her face. In the same way, we pair a word with its meaning or definition. We pair a car with the company that makes it (like Ford). When we hear a song, we think of its title. Sometimes forming pairs is called *association*; thus we may associate a name with a face. When we read about reading (Chapter 6), we will talk about sound-symbol association. This is the pairing of letters with sounds.

We are all different in our ability to pair things. Some of us have no trouble at all remembering a name when we see a face, and others have to struggle to attach names to faces. Some students are excellent at memorizing new vocabulary by filing away a word with its meaning and remembering the two together. Other students can spend hours and hours struggling to learn a list of vocabulary words and still do poorly on a test the next day. Everyone has strengths and weaknesses in pairing ability. To improve your understanding of your long-term memory performance, it is helpful to think about the kinds of things that you can pair easily and the kinds of pairs that don't work well in your mind.

Categories: Another way of organizing information in the long-term storage system is by groups, sometimes called categories. We might store all animals together. We would do this by putting them in a big "brain file cabinet" or "dresser," in a different place from where we would keep plants. Within the animal section we might separate insects and farm animals from pets (putting them in different drawers). We might then divide pets into more categories, including dogs, cats, birds, gerbils and tropical fish (putting them in different parts of the drawer).

We might then take the dogs and divide them into different breeds, such as Collies, German Shepherds, and Great Danes (arranging them side-by-side in the drawer). So then when we hear about a new breed of dog, we store that new information in the dog category, which is part of the pet category, which is part of the animal category. When we want to remember something about a particular pet, we can then go back through the drawers searching through the right drawer and the groups within the groups of animals to find the one we need to remember.

Chains: A third way of organizing material in memory is through chains. As you know, a chain is of a series of links; each link in a chain is attached to the one before it and the one after it. There are many things that are organized in memory as chains. A musician remembers how to play a particular tune because that tune was organized in memory as a chain. As he plays each note, he knows which note comes next in the chain. Cursive writing is organized as a chain. Each muscle movement shows you which muscle movement comes next in the chain of movements needed to form a letter. Other things that are organized in memory chains include the steps for solving certain kinds of mathematics problems, the steps in tying a shoelace, the chain of events in a story you want to remember, the sequence of months of the year, and the order of digits in your telephone number. Certain experiences are also organized in chains. For example, if you go on a field trip with your class, and you know you will have to write about what happened during the field trip, you might organize that trip as a chain of events in your mind. Then when you talk or write about the trip later, you just need to remember the chain. You might say, "First, we got on the bus; then we arrived at the museum. We then got out and walked around and saw all the prehistoric animals. When we finished seeing the animals, we went and had lunch. Then we got back to school just as it was closing."

Rules: A fourth way of organizing facts or skills in memory is through rules. Spelling rules are a good example. We might remember the rule "*i* before *e* except after *c*." There are also rules in grammar, mathematics, computers, science, and foreign languages. By learning the rules for something, we can remember it better. There are some students who are excellent at learning rules, while others seem to have their most trouble in subjects where there are many rules to be learned and remembered.

Storing Information in More Than One Way: Some of the best students remember skills and ideas well because they store them in more than one way. When they hear or see or think about a fact, they figure out how it might fit into many different pairs, groups, chains, or rules. When they need to remember that fact later on, there are several possible drawers in which to find it. It would be as if you wanted to remember the combination to a lock, so you wrote it down on three sheets of paper, and then put one copy in your wallet, one in your desk drawer, and one in your friend's locker. Then if you needed to find the combination, there would be several places to look. In the same way, if a social studies teacher were to mention the president of a country, you might store that person's name by making a pair between the president and the country, by putting him or her into a group called presidents and leaders around the world, by thinking about something you heard about that president on the news recently, and by putting the name within a group of others that sound or look similar. You could even make up a rule about the president, or try to use a chain by remembering which president came just before or after the one whose name you must remember now. In this way, the president's name would be stored in many different ways and should be much easier to locate when you need it. As we have said, good students seem to put information in several memory drawers. Other kids have less luck with memory because they keep putting ideas in only one place.

Elaboration: Elaboration can also help you organize ideas in memory. It involves talking about and thinking about an idea in many different ways. Kids who try to memorize without elaborating often have a harder time finding stored ideas when they need them later. Other kids are great elaborators. A good elaborator might hear about the planets and think about which one he would like to go to and what it would be like to fly there and what life there would be like. A non-elaborator might just try to memorize the names of the planets.

Finding Things in Memory

As you go through school, you need to get better and better at finding what you've stored in long-term memory. By the time you're in high school, you need to be a memory wizard. When you grow up, you actually need much less memory than you do in high school. As an adult with a job, you generally remember the same kinds of things every day. In school, when you're a kid, teachers and books present new information and skills every day. So your memory can get pretty exhausted by the time you reach sixteen or seventeen. It can also get stronger and stronger.

Recognition: One way to find things in your memory is to recognize them. If you see something familiar, you can say, "I recognize that" or "I've seen that before." Recognition is a pretty easy form of memory. You might recognize someone's face but not be able to think of his name. You might recognize a word but not be able to remember its definition.

Recall: Much of what happens in school requires recall, which is a different and more difficult kind of memory than recognition. To recall, you have to find within your memory an entire chunk of information with few or no clues. For example, you have to recall multiplication tables and spelling words. Often you have to recall information very fast. When you're taking a test or when you're called on in class, there's not much time to search in your memory. Also, you often have to recall several different things at the same time. When you write, you have to recall how to make letters, how to spell, how to punctuate, how to use good grammar, and what to capitalize. Doing all this at once puts a lot of strain on your memory. For some kids, recall is just too slow. It takes them too long to locate what they need. Other kids are good at recalling some kinds of information but not other kinds. A student may be very good at recalling the parts of engines but have trouble recalling the parts of speech.

Kinds of Recall: There are many kinds of recall. For example, there is the *recall of words*. When you want to say something, you need to be able to find the exact words you need quickly and accurately. There is also *visual recall*. When you want to recall what somebody's house looks like, you try to picture it in your memory. The recall of these visual images, as they are called, is also important for spelling. Another kind of recall is called *episodic memory*. It has to do with recalling things that have happened to you. There seems to be a special part of the brain for this kind of memory. It allows you to think about a television show you saw last week, where you were last December, and what places you visited two summers ago. Then there is a kind of recall called *procedural memory*. It has to do with how well you can recall how to do various things. Your procedural memory lets you recall how to tie your shoelaces, how to brush your teeth, how to ride a bicycle, and how to do division problems in arithmetic. Recall using procedural memory is very different from recall *memory for facts* that you learn like the capitals of different countries, important dates in history, and knowledge about plants and animals. In many subjects, you need both kinds of recall. For example, in mathematics, you need memory for facts (like $6 \times 7 = 42$), and you also need procedural memory for using the facts (like recalling how to multiply with four digits).

Automatic Memory: Sometimes recall works so fast that you can recall things without even trying to or thinking very hard. By fifth or sixth grade, you have to solve math problems quickly, so you can't take a long time to recall that $3 + 4 = 7$ or that $4 \times 2 = 8$. These facts must come out automatically from your memory drawers. Some students have trouble recalling automatically. It might take them an extra year or two to get the multiplication tables into their automatic memory or to be able to get letters to flow through a pencil so quickly and smoothly that they don't have to think about them while they're writing.

Students who are delayed in getting automatic memory (sometimes called automaticity) to work for them often have a very hard time in school.

Keeping Things Together

As we observed at the beginning of this chapter, memory is not used simply to store and find what we see, hear, or think about. Memory is also used to "hold things together" while we are working on them. To understand this idea, you might imagine that in order to think you need something like a television screen in your mind. Now imagine what it would be like to watch television if different parts of the screen kept disappearing while you were watching an exciting mystery. Most of the time you could see only part of the screen. To make matters worse, let's pretend that the sound wasn't very good either, that it kept fading on and off. Meanwhile, you would be struggling to understand what the show was about. You would certainly get confused. You might also start to "tune out" and daydream or to try to find something else to do. That is just what happens to some students who have a lot of trouble keeping things on the working "screens" in their minds while they are listening, thinking, writing, or doing math problems in school.

Active Working Memory: The memory that you need to keep things together on your working screen is called active working memory. There are plenty of students who have trouble with this kind of memory. When they do arithmetic problems, some of them have trouble remembering what they are supposed to do while they are doing the problem! For example, a student might be carrying a number in a multiplication problem. While carrying that number, she might forget what she was going to do after she carried the number. Other students may have forgotten the beginning of a paragraph by the time they get to the end of it. This makes it hard for them to remember (and also to understand) what they read. Somehow, their active working memory screens do not hold onto things well. There is too much fading out while they are working. One boy who had this problem said that he understands arithmetic but gets "wiped out" on tests. When asked what happens in his mind when he tries to do math problems, he just said, "Scrambled eggs." He meant that things get all mixed up. His active working memory screen loses parts of what he is doing while he is doing it!

It is possible to have a good active working memory while doing certain kinds of things but not while doing others. Some students have trouble keeping everything on their screens when they read, but are good at holding things there when they do arithmetic. Others may have trouble holding enough in memory while they are copying from the board. Some students have real problems with active working memory when they write. When they try to think of a word they want to use, they forget what sentence they were going to put it in. This is too bad, since often these same kids have excellent ideas. Somehow their great thoughts get lost while they are trying to organize and write out a paragraph.

Active working memory is also important in sports. A basketball player needs to be able to think about many things at the same time. For example, while dribbling, the player must remember where the other players are, decide whether or not to shoot, and recall rules, such as the one that says you can't stop and then start dribbling the ball again. A good basketball player can keep all of those things (and more) on his or her

"Now, class, take out your pencils and copy. . . ."

Some students have trouble holding enough material in memory while they are copying from the chalkboard. They cannot store in their minds a large enough "chunk" of words, so they have to look up too often while they copy. They can then lose their place and take too long to copy from the board.

active working memory screen while playing. A not-so-good basketball player would forget a particular rule while dribbling.

You can see that memory is crucial because it affects so many different kinds of learning. As we have said, memory often needs to be fast. It needs to be accurate. Plus, you have to be able to recall several different things at the same time. As you go through school, more and more of your memory is supposed to become automatic so it can be very fast and easy to use. Also, the more often you recall something, the easier it becomes to recall it. In using memory, as in many other things we do, "Practice makes perfect!" Practice also makes memory work easier.

Since there are many different types of memory, it's no wonder that nobody has a totally good or totally bad memory. When someone is talking about memory, you have to ask, "What kind of memory are you talking about?" It would be a good idea, at this point, for you to think about your own memory strengths and weaknesses. If you look at the chart that begins on this page and continues onto page 74, you will see a review of the different kinds of memory.

Some of the Many Kinds of Memory
(Don't try to remember all of these.)

Kind of Memory	Description	Example
Visual Memory	Memory for what you've seen	Remembering what someone looks like
Auditory Memory	Memory for what you've heard	Remembering some directions the teacher gave you
Sequential Memory	Memory for things in a certain order	Remembering the digits in a telephone number
Short-Term Memory	Recent Memory	Remembering directions you just heard

Kind of Memory	Description	Example
Long-Term Memory	Memory for things you learned a long time ago	Remembering the multiplication tables for years and years
Recognition Memory	Memory for knowing that something is familiar	Remembering you know someone when you see her
Recall or Retrieval Memory	Finding stored facts and skills that you need when you need them	Remembering how to spell during a spelling bee
Automatic Memory	Memory that is so fast you don't have to think much to remember what you need	Remembering how to form letters while you write
Episodic Memory	Memory for things that have happened in your life	Remembering the good time you had at the beach you went to last summer
Procedural Memory	Memory for how to do things	Remembering how to do a multiplication problem
Motor Memory	Memory for how to do things with your muscles	Remembering how to ride a bicycle
Factual Memory	Memory for knowledge	Remembering the names of the planets
Active Working Memory	Memory for keeping things together in your mind while you need them	Remembering the directions for a report while you're writing it

WHAT YOU CAN DO ABOUT MEMORY PROBLEMS

Fortunately, there is a lot that can be done to work on a memory problem in school. We will mention some ideas, but students need to come up with their own ideas too. Remember, everybody has some problems with some kinds of memory. So everybody needs some improvement. But some students need improvement more than others.

Know How Memory Works

Kids who know something about how memory is supposed to work will find it easier to know if and when memory is causing a problem for them. (Most students with memory problems don't even know that they have these problems!) Those who do think that they may have a memory problem often don't know what kind of problem they have. But unless someone knows exactly what the trouble is, he or she will not be able to fix the problem. Students can find out more about strengths and weaknesses in their memory in several ways. These include talking with parents and other adults, using this book, and possibly taking some special tests.

Know Which Memory Jobs You're Doing

To make memory work well, it helps to know which of the memory jobs you're doing at any time. For example, you can ask yourself, "Am I registering? Am I putting facts away for later use? Am I trying to dig something out of memory right now? Or am I trying to hold things together in my mind while I work on them?" In other words, you have to be aware or conscious of your memory. You can't ignore it, and you can't believe that it will work on "automatic pilot" all the time. The truth is that your memory needs instructions from you. In Chapter 2, we talked about attention and how it needs to be controlled from "the cockpit." Now we can say that memory needs someone to manage it. So it is always important to think about your memory while you are using it and to know which memory job you are doing or which memory job you are about to do.

Use Strategies

As a student you have to invent and use good memory strategies. Strategies are techniques or methods for doing things the best and easiest way. A physician has to come up with some strategies to cure an illness. When a coach wants to win a soccer game, he or she is likely to sit down with the team and talk about some strategies to defeat the other team.

There are many different kinds of strategies that can be used to make your memory more of a winner too.

One strategy is called the *rehearsal* strategy. Rehearsal is a way of registering new things in memory with enough depth of processing. Just as actors and actresses rehearse to remember their lines, you can rehearse things you want to store. If you have to memorize some spelling words, you can rehearse them by whispering them under your breath or saying them out loud while you read them. Another way to rehearse is to make a visual picture in your brain as you read each word. You can also rehearse by reading the spelling word, then writing it, and then whispering the correct spelling to yourself. Rehearsal improves registration through greater depth of processing.

There are also *grouping* strategies that can help you get things organized in long-term storage so you can find them later. We have already discussed how you can make pairs, chains, or groups of things. The more carefully you do that, and the more different kinds of groups or pairs you can make, the more likely it is you will remember what you need to later. Coming up with original groups and pairs that are interesting, fun, or funny is another kind of memory strategy. It is one way to elaborate on new ideas or facts.

There are also *association* strategies for finding things in your memory. If you are having trouble recalling, a strategy would be to think about things that are like what you are trying to remember. If you can't recall someone's name, think of other people who know him or who have been places with you and him and try to remember their names. Then you might find *his* name.

Problems with active working memory require excellent *study* strategies. If things keep fading from your memory screen, you need to concentrate very hard while you are working. One strategy would be to write down much more on paper. For example, in arithmetic, you probably should not do too many steps of a problem in your head. You should write down as much as possible. If you have trouble remembering the beginning of a paragraph when you are reading the end of it, use another strategy. You can underline the important parts at the beginning. Then, when you come to the end of each paragraph, you can read over what you underlined earlier. If you can't mark up your books, you can jot down key ideas or read them into a tape recorder.

Sometimes when you are having trouble with memory, it is important to reduce some of its load through *bypass* strategies. These are ways of working around a memory problem. If you are having difficulty remembering while you are doing mathe-

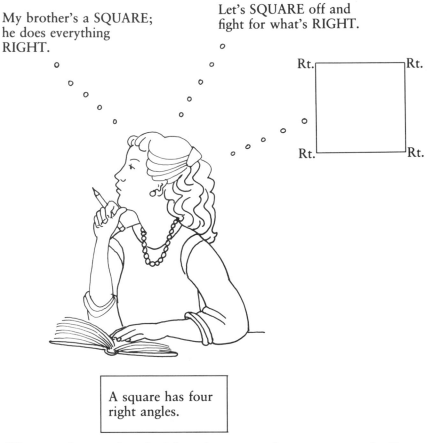

My brother's a SQUARE; he does everything RIGHT.

Let's SQUARE off and fight for what's RIGHT.

A square has four right angles.

"How can I remember that? I need some good memory strategies."

This girl is trying to remember the fact that a square has four right angles in it. She is using various memory strategies to be sure that she won't forget this important fact in geometry.

matics, you may need to ask your teacher if you can use a calculator at least some of the time. A word processor can help if it is hard for you to remember while you write. Some students who are having memory problems need to become excellent notetakers. They need to write down as much as possible. If you think about it, you can figure out ways to reduce the load on your memory. Often you can do things in such a way that your memory doesn't have to work so hard.

A Strategy for Studying for Tests

Having a good understanding of how your memory works (and doesn't work), can help you come up with the best strategy for studying for tests. At any rate, you should always have a memory plan (a kind of strategy) in your mind or on paper before you even begin studying.

To make a memory plan, you need to ask the following questions.

1. **What material will be covered on this test?**

2. **What is *most likely* to be asked on this test?** In other words, what are the most important things to know? As you go through school, you need to get better and better at predicting what you are going to be asked. If you become a good predictor, you won't have to work your memory quite as hard.

3. **What do I need to memorize, and what will I be able to figure out from what I know?** Not everything needs to be stored in memory. Some things can be thought about during a test.

4. **What's the best strategy for me to use to rehearse and store what I will need to know for the test?** Can I come up with any clever strategies for memorizing? For example, should I dictate the most important ideas onto a tape and then play them back? Should I make charts or lists or diagrams?

5. **How much time should I allow to store what I need to store?** Remember, when figuring out how much time it will take to load up your memory, you need to figure in some breaks. No one can work non-stop! Also, it is important to find the time of day or night that you study best.

6. **What study strategies can I use so that I will know when I know enough?** In other words, how can I test myself so I can find out if I'm finished with my memory work? Some students use flash cards. Others try to get a sample test to take. Some get together with classmates, and they quiz each other. That can work unless you start fooling around too much and talking about things that have nothing to do with the test.

If you write down your plan, you should check off each part as you finish it. Finally, when you get back a test, it is important to review your answers very carefully. It is especially good to check out your mistakes and to see whether your memory plan was a good one or not. For example, you should ask yourself, "Did I study the right things or not?" Also, you should check each mistake to see whether it was a mistake of memory, of understanding, or of carelessness. Doing this should help you decide on the best memory strategies.

SOME FINAL ADVICE ABOUT REMEMBERING

Many students get very nervous or tense when they're having trouble recalling something. Unfortunately, the more "uptight" you become, the harder it is to recall anything. So, if you really want to help your memory work well, you have to "hang in there," keep concentrating, and stay calm. If you're having trouble recalling on a test, you shouldn't give up, you shouldn't get too scared, and you shouldn't guess right away. Instead, relax and think up strategies to use. Use as many different strategies as you can to search for the right answer.

Deep in every brain, there's a huge "lost and found." Get good at using your memory's lost and found. You have to be flexible and persistent. If you can't remember how to spell a word, try to picture it. If you can't picture it, sound it out. If that doesn't work, write down several spelling versions and see which one looks best. If that doesn't work, try to think of similar words and how they're spelled. That's good use of your lost and found. The point is: if something doesn't come to you right away, keep searching for it.

Probably the most important lesson you can learn from this chapter is that as you go through school, you need to learn not only about reading, social studies, and other subjects, but also about learning and memory. At the same time that you are trying to improve your reading, for example, you can also be trying to improve your memory.

Now that we have discussed many ideas about memory, we can examine another brain function, the uses of language.

CHAPTER FOUR

A Code Called Language

SUE'S STORY

Sue hates school. She gets embarrassed all the time. When teachers call on her, she can never quite figure out what to say. She has good ideas, but she has trouble putting them into words and sentences. Although she has a pretty good vocabulary, she can't think up the right words fast enough to answer when she is asked a question. She has just as much trouble getting her ideas onto paper, so her reports and tests are not very good. Everyone knows she is intelligent, but everyone is disappointed in what she says and writes. Sue also has some trouble understanding other people when they talk fast or in long sentences.

Sometimes Sue feels completely lost in class. The teacher will be explaining something, and Sue just can't follow it. When this happens, she often "tunes out" and starts thinking about other things like music or her cats. However, Sue is good in some kinds of math—everything except word prob-

lems. She can never figure out what to do when she reads one.

Although Sue is excellent at reading out loud, she has trouble understanding and remembering what she has read. Because of this trouble, she hates to read. In fact, she is starting to dislike school because it requires so much reading and listening and answering.

While much of school is difficult for Sue, there are some things in her life that come easily for her. She is an excellent musician. She plays the clarinet and actually writes music. She has taken music lessons, and her clarinet teacher thinks she is very talented. She's also super at sports and great with computers.

Sue doesn't have many friends. She is very quiet and shy. Nobody seems to dislike her or make fun of her. But hardly anyone seems to know her very well. Her parents feel that Sue is shy and quiet because she cannot keep up with other kids when they talk a lot. The few kids who get to know her say they really like her. They realize that she's a neat kid, even though she doesn't say too much.

Thinking More about Sue

Try answering the following questions about Sue after reading all of Chapter 4.

- What are the ways in which Sue's problems are making life hard for her?
- How will it help Sue if she knows that she has language problems?

THE LANGUAGE CODE

A code is something we use so that others can understand what we are saying or writing and so that we can understand what they are saying or writing. Codes are not understood by everyone. In fact, by putting ideas into a code, we can decide who will understand them and who will not. You probably know about secret codes used by armies or by spies. Maybe you, like many kids, have made up a secret code just for fun.

Human beings have a code that we use all the time. This code is called language. Like other codes, some people can understand and use the language code very well, others not so well, and still others not at all. Our language code is called English, and we become good at figuring it out and using it. People in some other countries have their own codes, like French, Spanish, Russian, Chinese, or German. Most of us would have trouble using or understanding all of those codes.

In any school there are students who are excellent with the English language code. There are others who have good ideas but who have trouble putting these ideas into words or figuring out other people's ideas from their words. It is possible to be a person with excellent ideas and thoughts and yet have trouble with the language code. Students with language disorders can have a very hard time in school. In order to understand why this is so, we will review the ways language affects your success as a student.

The Uses of Language

Understanding and Communicating: Unless you're a mind reader, it is hard to know what someone is thinking if he or she doesn't use the language code to tell you. Sometimes you can get a few hints by looking carefully at the person. The expression on someone's face may tell you that she is confused, angry, sad, or happy. Even the position of a person's body can give you hints about how he feels or what he may be thinking. When people talk or write in the language code, they are letting you know their thoughts and feelings. You can then compare their words and sentences with your own feelings, memories, and ideas.

We can see that two important uses of language are understanding and describing (sometimes called communicating). In a conversation, we usually take turns understanding and describing. First, you may say something to someone. (This is *describing*.) Then, that person tries to understand what you said. Next, he or she says something back to you (*describing*) that you need to understand. If you understand, you can then say something about what the other person has just said.

Understanding is sometimes called *receptive* language. It is called receptive because it has to do with a person's ability to receive other people's ideas through the language code. The parts of your brain that take in the language code (mostly in the temporal lobe) are like the receiver of a telephone, the part that goes up against your ear. Such a receiver receives language-coded information from the wires that lead to the phone. In the same way, the receptive language parts of your brain receive language that comes from other people.

Expressive language is like the transmitter, the part of the telephone near your mouth. Expressive language has to do with communicating—getting your own ideas into language so other people can receive your ideas.

Thinking: Language is also important for thinking. Just about everyone does a lot of his or her thinking in words and sentences. Whether we're trying to solve an arithmetic problem or thinking about what we'll do next weekend, we often find it much easier to think with language. On the other hand, some people are good at thinking without language. Someone might fix a computer

Some students with receptive language difficulties have trouble understanding long or complicated sentences. Somehow, reception is poor for them. They may need the teacher to talk slowly or to repeat some of what was said because otherwise the message is too "blurry" for them.

by looking carefully at all of its parts and figuring out what doesn't look right. That kind of thinking may not require any words or sentences either spoken aloud or thought about in the mind. Some students are very good at thinking without language, while others use the language code for just about all of their thinking. But everybody uses language some of the time for thinking.

Remembering: The language code also helps us remember things. Many facts and ideas are registered in memory in the form of words and sentences. Sometimes, when we try to memorize things like spelling words or rules, we actually repeat them out loud (which, as we saw in the last chapter, is a good memory strategy). It is easier to register certain ideas by putting them into words and sentences. It is easier to put facts in the right memory drawers by first describing them in language—either out loud or under your breath—and then storing them in a language code. It is also true that we remember people by remembering their names. A person's name becomes the code for that person.

Social Life: Language is also important for social life. We all use language to make and keep friends. In many schools, kids feel that they have to talk a certain way to be well liked. They may have to use particular words in a particular way at a particular time to be considered particularly "cool." You have to be good at using language to know how to joke around, to know when to say things that make other kids feel good, and to be able to express ideas that will help your friends like you. If you are good at social language, you can use language as one way to form and keep strong relationships. We will talk more about language as a social skill in Chapter 7.

Talking to Yourself: You may not realize it, but language is used for talking to yourself just as much as it's used for talking to other people. Throughout the day, all of us talk to ourselves. That doesn't mean we're crazy. Some of what we say helps us think better. Other things we say to ourselves cheer us on, organize us, and sometimes even criticize us so that we'll perform better in the future. For example, while playing a sport, an athlete may say to herself, "You'd better keep your eye on the ball or you're going to miss this one." Another athlete may say to himself, "Keep it up. You're doing great. Just hang in there. You're a superstar today!" Talking to yourself can be very helpful, especially if what you say encourages you, makes you feel good, and reminds you to continue concentrating.

It's too bad that some people always put themselves down when they talk to themselves. There are students who say discouraging things to themselves while they're taking tests. They look at test questions and say to themselves, "You'll never be

---

Students who are good at the language functions listed below have an excellent chance of doing well in school. Those who have trouble with one or more of these uses have to struggle to get good grades.

1. Understanding the ideas of others
2. Communicating their own ideas
3. Thinking
4. Remembering
5. Making and keeping friends
6. Talking to themselves

---

able to do this. This is too hard. You've had it. Just give up." That kind of talking to yourself can make you fail even when you study hard. A student who finds himself discouraging himself like this should try to change his inner language and be more of a cheerleader! You need to encourage yourself when you talk to yourself. You need to tell yourself: "That looks hard, but I can do it. I've been able to do it before. I'll just keep at it; I won't give up. This is going to be a good day."

Confusion over Language

Kids who have language disorders find language confusing. Next, we will discuss some things about language that can confuse students.

What's a Language Sound and What's Not: As sounds pass through your ears and into the language-interpreting parts of the brain, your mind must decide which of the sounds are language sounds and which are not. The sound of a door closing is not language. The sound of a dog barking is not language. (At least it's not *your* language.) The sound of a person coughing or sneezing is not language. However, words and sentences are made up entirely of language sounds. Different languages have different sounds in them. People who understand Chinese are aware of a long list of language sounds that are different from the ones we know in English. As a very young baby, you learn which of all the sounds entering your brain are language sounds from your language and which are not.

Sounds That Are Similar but Not Exactly the Same: Once you learn to recognize and pronounce the sounds within your language, you quickly realize that some sounds are similar to each other, while others are very different from each other. It's not too difficult to tell the difference in sound between the word *cold* and the word *hot*. But it may not be easy to notice the difference between the words *cold* and *code*—especially if you have a cold! Words like these cause some students to have serious problems. Somehow, their brains don't give them a clear idea of the differences between sounds that are similar. These students often develop major problems with reading and spelling. Both of these skills require a strong appreciation or sense of the specialness of English language sounds. This way you can store them in your memory paired with certain combinations of letters.

"Was that *ball* or *bowl*?"

Some students get confused about language sounds. A kid with a language disorder may sometimes have trouble telling similar sounds apart when he hears them or reads them. This is what's disturbing this bewildered boy.

Growth of Vocabulary: Another challenge for understanding language is vocabulary growth. The size of a person's vocabulary has to do with how many words he or she can understand and/or use. It is really amazing how many words kids understand even when they are very young. In the earliest grades of school, most kids know about 2,000 to 3,000 words, and most likely they learn new words almost every day. These words are stored in the vocabulary drawers of memory, so when someone listens, he or she compares what is heard to what memory indicates the words mean.

Most word learning takes place by hearing or reading a word and figuring out what it must mean from the way it's used. But, some vocabulary gets learned by studying. As we said in the last chapter, some students find learning new words to be fun and easy. Memorizing a list of new vocabulary words and their definitions is no problem at all for these students. For other kids, learning new words is boring and hard. (Incidentally, jobs that seem too hard have a way of becoming boring.) Memorizing a list of words for these kids is torture. They can't stand this kind of assignment. Sometimes they do everything possible to avoid vocabulary study. So, some students end up with large vocabularies, while others have small vocabularies.

How Words Can Change When a Few Letters Change: Whenever we learn a new word, we need to find out all of the different things that can be done to it. For example, we learn about letters that can be added at the beginning or end of the word (prefixes and suffixes). These letter combinations can tell you whether something is singular (like *cat*) or plural (like *cats*). Other letter combinations show whether a word is in the past or present tense. A student with language problems might get confused about these different groups of letters that change words to give them different meanings. (The study of the way letters get added to words to change them is called *morphology*.)

The Order of Words: Once we have a good knowledge of many words (including their prefixes and suffixes), we still have the job of arranging or understanding these words in groups. We need to know how to make phrases (little groups of words) and sentences. To make sentences out of words, you need to understand

DIRECT
DIRECTS
DIRECTED
DIRECTION
DIRECTIVE
DIRECTOR
DIRECTORS

The understanding of word forms, or morphology, is an important part of language. In this example, a teacher is pointing out many different word forms based on the root word direct. *Being able to use or understand multiple word forms made from the same root is an important part of language ability.*

how to put words in the correct order. The correct order is called the *syntax*.

The order of words in a sentence can have a lot to do with the meaning of that sentence. For example, the sentence "The boy followed the robber all the way to his home" is very different from the sentence "The robber followed the boy all the way to his home." In the first sentence, the boy is helping to catch a thief. In the second sentence, the thief is out to get the boy. Actually, the order of words in the sentence is crucial!

Some kids with language problems have trouble arranging words in the best order, or they may have trouble understanding the order of words in a sentence that they hear or read.

What's Grammatical and What's Not: In addition to getting the order of words right, you should use good grammar, too. Every language has sentences that are built correctly for that language. These good sentences are said to be "grammatical." A sentence such as "Them people ain't got no good manners" is not grammatical. Part of being good with language is having the ability to understand and use the special rules that are part of your language's code. These rules tell you the grammatical ways to put your ideas into words. It is grammatical to say, "Those people don't have good manners." Some students find language rules so natural that they almost never have to think about them. Other kids find the rules of language really hard to remember and understand. They have trouble knowing what is grammatical and what is not grammatical.

Understanding and Using Narratives: Narratives are groups of sentences that are connected to each other. They describe or tell us about something by putting sentences together in the right order so they make sense. Words like *then, because,* and *before* tie sentences together so that they sound smooth and connected. Otherwise, the language may sound like just a list of sentences or phrases.

It is important to understand other people's narratives or

"The horse that was chased by the dog ran away. The dog chasing the horse ran away. After being chased by the horse, the dog ran away."

This girl is having fun thinking up many different ways of arranging words in a sentence. She is realizing how important syntax (word order) really is. Her ideas about the relationship between the horse and the dog will depend upon the order of the words she uses to talk about them.

passages. A person must also be able to create his or her own narratives or passages. To make your own, you need to be able to organize ideas in words and sentences. Then you must put those words and sentences in the correct order. You also need to know what the listener knows. That means that you have to think all the time about the person you're talking to. You shouldn't use words that are too hard, and you shouldn't talk about people that the other person doesn't know without telling him who they are. If you don't give enough information, the person you're talking to may get confused.

To understand a narrative or passage, you need to be able to listen well and remember what has just been said. Some kids seem to have trouble listening, remembering, and thinking all at the same time. This is the case especially among students with language disorders. They may become confused when a teacher or someone else talks for a long time. Big "chunks" of language are often too much for them.

Inferring: Language comprehension is absolutely necessary in many aspects of our lives. As we have seen, understanding or comprehending language involves being good in all of the different parts of language we have discussed. It also includes the ability to think about language. Often we have to think hard about what somebody really means. Sometimes the true meaning is hidden and we have to figure it out. For example, take the following two sentences: "Mary and Susie love to play with each other every day after school. However, each night just before they go to sleep, they argue a lot." If you read just the first sentence, you would probably decide that Mary and Susie are simply very good friends. However, after you read the second sentence, you may want to change your mind. It starts to sound as if Mary and Susie are sisters, since they seem to be together every night at bedtime. Yet, nowhere in those two sentences did the speaker ever say that Mary and Sue were sisters. You had to figure that out. Figuring out things like this is called *inferring*. It is a very important part of understanding language. It has to do with using clues to fill in missing information by thinking while you're listening or reading. Many important ideas are never said directly. They are implied or partly hidden. That means that a really good language interpreter must also be a skilled language thinker. Some students are much better at language thinking and at thinking about language than are others.

WHAT IT'S LIKE TO HAVE A LANGUAGE DISORDER

You can see from what we have said so far that ability with language is important in school. Kids whose language skills are weak compared to others of their age can have serious problems as students. Even though they are very intelligent in other important ways (and most of them are), students with language disorders are apt to find school especially difficult and sometimes frustrating and embarrassing.

Possible Problems

Students with language problems are not all the same. Some are poor at certain parts of language but not at other parts. Also, the effects of language disorders will depend upon a lot of other things. These include the student's ability to concentrate and his or her other strengths and weaknesses.

Here is a list of the kinds of problems that kids with language disorders *might* have.

1. **Understanding spoken instructions:** Some students with language problems feel a teacher is talking too fast. They get mixed up when a teacher gives complicated instructions or explanations.

2. **Vocabulary:** Some kids with language problems are slow at learning, understanding, and using new words. Because of this, they are always behind in vocabulary.

3. **Reading:** Students with language disorders may find themselves far behind in reading. In first and second grade, some students may have trouble sounding out or identifying individual words because of a poor appreciation of language sounds. Other kids may be able to appreciate the sounds, but they have trouble remembering them. As school goes on, such students often have more and more difficulty with understanding or remembering what was read. (We will talk more about reading problems in Chapter 6.)

4. **Expressing ideas in words:** Some kids with language problems have a good enough vocabulary, but it is too hard for them to recall, or find, the right words quickly when they need them. Such students may have trouble participating in class discussions. Some kids say they get very nervous and uptight when they are called on in class. Although they often know the right answers, it's hard for them to find the exact words and say the sentences accurately and quickly enough.

This kind of expressive language problem can be very embarrassing. One girl said: "I have good ideas, but whenever I say my ideas they come out sounding dumb." That girl did, in fact, have excellent ideas, but it was too much of a long, hard struggle for her to get those ideas into good English sentences. She was often embarrassed in class because of her problem. Yet, she was excellent at fixing things and a smart person in so many other ways.

5. **Writing and spelling:** Some students who are poor at expressing their ideas have just as much trouble getting those ideas down on paper. Compositions, book reports, stories, and other writing assignments are a huge problem for them. Some kids have problems with spelling. Often, these kids don't have a good sense of the sounds of the language. They may spell words that look like the real thing. But those words have combinations of letters in them that are not really part of English. For example, a student may spell the word *light* as *laght*. These two spellings look similar, but there is no way to pronounce *laght* in English. *Laght* may look almost right, but it surely doesn't sound right!

6. **Word problems and teachers' explanations in mathematics:** Many students with language problems do well in math because they are good at reasoning, visualizing, and problem solving. But some parts of math require you to understand teachers' explanations through language. Also, solving word problems requires a good understanding of language. Explanations and word problems may cause trouble for some students with language disorders.

7. **Learning a second language:** A student with a language disorder in his or her own language can find it especially hard

to learn a foreign language. So, some kids who have even very mild language problems in English get into real difficulty when they have to take a second language.

8. **Remembering language:** There are some students who have trouble remembering things that come into their brains coded in language. They have verbal memory problems. (See page 59.) It is hard for them to remember instructions and other important things people have said. They may also have a hard time remembering what they've read.

9. **Social difficulties:** Some students with language problems have trouble making friends and being popular. This is partly because they are not very skilled at using language with other people. Without realizing it, they may say things that disturb or annoy others. They may choose words or use a tone of voice that makes them sound angry when they really don't feel angry. Some students cannot quite "talk the same language" as other kids, and so they may seem weird. We will talk more about this and other kinds of social abilities in Chapter 7.

WHAT CAN BE DONE ABOUT LANGUAGE DISORDERS?

A lot can be done to help kids with language disorders. First, of course, the student must realize that he or she is having difficulties with the language code in school. Once students realize what their problem is, they can often come up with many excellent things to do so that the problem doesn't cause too much trouble for them.

Identify Problems and Their Effects in School

In order to help a student with language problems, it is important to know what kinds of language problems the student has. It is also important to know how those language problems are actually affecting what goes on in school. Is the language weakness interfering with reading? Is it making it hard to follow directions? Is it causing problems with friends? These are the kinds of questions that need to be answered before it is possible to figure out ways of working on the problem.

Get Help from Teachers

A teacher needs to know that a student has a language disorder. Sometimes the teacher needs to be careful not to talk too quickly or in sentences that are too long. Sometimes the teacher needs to give a student some visual material to illustrate what is being said. Often, a student with a language disorder needs to sit close to the teacher so that he or she can listen better. If a student has a hard time finding words and talking in a class discussion, there is something that the teacher can do to help. She can ask the student only questions that can be answered with a "yes" or a "no."

Use Strengths To Make Up for Weaknesses

Many students with language disorders are very good at picturing things. Their visual abilities (which we will talk about in the next chapter) are strong. Sometimes they are talented in art or in designing, inventing, or fixing things. Many are excellent at thinking up projects that don't involve a lot of words, sentences, or long passages. Such students need to use their nonlanguage strengths to help themselves with language. Whenever possible, they need to be attaching words and sentences to pictures. For example, some students with language problems are helped by reading comic books. These same students find something like model building easier when the instructions contain a lot of visual clues to help with language comprehension. Some older students learn that they have to make diagrams, lists, charts, and drawings to illustrate what they are reading in a textbook. By translating a chapter into visual material, they are helping themselves understand and remember what they have read. They can then use the visual materials to study for quizzes or tests.

Get Help from Others

Students with language disorders may need extra help with reading, writing, and spelling. The tutor who does this should understand a student's language problems as well as his or her strengths in certain parts of language or in other areas.

Some kids with language disorders can get help from a speech and language therapist. This is a person who has been specially trained to work with people who are having difficulties understanding or communicating. A language therapist can also help a classroom teacher to understand a student's language difficulties. Many schools have language therapists, and it is also possible to get language help outside of school.

Don't Get Discouraged

Kids with language disorders should not get discouraged. Many of them improve steadily as they go through school. However, there are some students who get behind in school because of their language problems. They get too discouraged and do as little schoolwork as possible. Because they do so little school-work, they get too little practice with language. This means that their language skills end up further behind those of kids who get a lot of practice through schoolwork. The moral of the story is that students with language problems need to keep working hard. They mustn't allow themselves to get discouraged or their language problems will get worse.

CHAPTER FIVE

Some Other Important Brain Functions

TANYA'S STORY

Tanya is very popular. She has a pleasing personality and very good looks. Her phone is always ringing with invitations to go to parties or calls just to chat. She loves dancing, playing the guitar, and singing, but school has not been too pleasant for Tanya.

Although she wants to do well, she has found some subjects extremely difficult. This frustrates her because she'd love to go on to college. She often visits her brother at the university he attends. She thinks that he and his friends are really neat and that college looks like a lot of fun. But she wonders if she'll ever get there. Her grades have been going down steadily.

Tanya's parents think that she doesn't try very hard, but Tanya disagrees. She believes that she does try and that trying does not do any good. She feels that her school problems are pretty much out of her control.

Tanya's teachers observe that she always has interesting things to say; however, they have also noticed that she has trouble following directions. When she's given more than one thing to do at a time, she just plain forgets what to do. She also has trouble doing things in the right order. When faced with a math problem, she gets mixed up about what to do first, what to do second, and what to do after that. She had a lot of trouble learning the multiplication tables, and even now she is slow to remember them. Compared to other children, Tanya was late in learning how to tell time, and she is still mixed up about the months of the year. She can't remember whether March comes before April or whether April comes before March.

Tanya's teachers feel that she has difficulty with sequences. This means that anything that has to be understood or re-membered in the right order causes trouble for her. As time passes, this trouble increases, because each year in school Tanya is expected to remember more sequences and longer sequences. Plus, teachers give her more activities that require her to do things in sequence. Of course, when she writes reports, she has to organize her ideas in the right order. This is extremely hard for her.

In school, Tanya gets special help in a resource room. This bothers her because it makes her feel different or weird, and she wants to be like everyone else. But she knows that the special teacher has been helping her a lot, and if she doesn't get help, she'll get further and further behind in school. Then she'd really feel weird! Besides, Tanya has noticed that since she has been going for help, other students have not really noticed or cared. She is just as popular as ever.

Thinking More about Tanya

Try answering the following questions after reading Chapter 5.

- Why is school getting harder and harder for Tanya?
- What kind of learning disorder makes it difficult to follow directions and learn the months of the year?
- Why does Tanya feel nervous about getting help? Is it common to feel this way?

NICK'S STORY

Nick can't stand writing assignments. They take too long, and his writing is a mess. He has always had trouble controlling a pencil—he can't hold it the way other kids do. When he writes, his hand seems to tense up. If he writes much, it feels as if his hand is aching. He holds the pencil very close to the point and straight up and down. It is as if his pencil is part of his fist. Sometimes it looks as if he is going to punch someone with his pencil! Nick insists that this is the only way he can write.

Despite Nick's writing problems, he has a terrific imagination and many exciting ideas about every subject in school. He can talk like a genius about science, history, and current events. He collects rocks and loves animals. He has three dogs, four cats, a snake, and two ferrets. Although Nick knows a tremendous amount about animals and nature, his super ideas don't "come across" on paper. What he writes is pretty poor compared to what he knows and thinks.

When Nick has to write a report, he feels like quitting school. He makes the report as short as possible because writing is so difficult for him. While he is making letters, he has trouble knowing where in the letter his pencil is! Sometimes he even has to watch his fingers very closely as he writes. This is so he can see, for example, that his pencil is at the top of a g and ready to come down again. Most people can tell where their fingers are without looking, but Nick can't. Nick also has trouble moving his fingers quickly to form letters easily. He has some of his biggest problems with ball point pens; they are too slippery for him. He does better with mechanical pencils, although he sometimes breaks the points because he bears down so hard.

Nick had some tests to find out why his writing is such a problem. It was found that he has a fine motor problem. His brain has trouble organizing muscle movements in his fingers quickly and accurately. Also, his brain doesn't keep track of where his fingers are during writing. When Nick's parents got the results of the tests, they were confused. They wondered how he could have a fine motor problem and be so good at fixing things, at drawing, and at building models. But then they were told that Nick has a kind of fine motor problem that disturbs only writing. They learned that other things that hands do don't require such fast use of the small finger muscles.

Nick is good at the kind of job where you have to study something with your eyes and then use your hands to fix or change it. This kind of visual-motor activity is not a problem for him. Nick also has no trouble getting his large muscles to work accurately and quickly, which is why he's so excellent at sports. It's only the small muscles in his fingers that give him a hard time when they have to work quickly and accurately, and the only time they need to do that is when he writes. Nick's best friend Sam seems to have the opposite problem. Sam is a great writer but has real trouble playing sports. His muscles just don't cooperate when he has to catch a ball, run, or kick.

Recently Nick's teachers have allowed him to use a word processor and this has helped him tremendously. His reports are neater. He can do them, and he can concentrate on having good ideas because he doesn't have to think about forming letters. Yet, Nick knows he can't give up on writing. He still needs to practice it so he can take notes and do well on tests. But, at least, the word processor helps him some of the time while he is working on his writing speed. He feels pretty sure that the more he practices writing, the easier it will get.

Thinking More about Nick

Try answering the following questions after reading Chapter 5.

- How is it possible for Nick to have trouble writing neatly when he does other things with his hands so well?
- How can Nick start to write better?
- Would it be good for Nick not to have to think up good ideas *while* writing? Should he think first (for example, on a cassette recorder) and write afterwards?

FOUR MORE BRAIN FUNCTIONS

This chapter will cover more brain functions that affect learning. These functions are abilities that the brain has to solve problems and help us do the best possible work in school. We also will see how these functions can create problems for some students. The functions that we will discuss in this chapter are 1) Visual-Spatial Ability, 2) Sequencing Ability, 3) Motor Functions, and 4) Thinking.

VISUAL-SPATIAL FUNCTIONS

Visual-spatial ability gives us information about the positions of things in space, about shapes and how they differ from each other, and about the size of objects. For example, our visual-spatial abilities allow us to see where a ball is in space so that we can catch it. A brain that is good at handling visual-spatial information can recognize that a picture on a particular page is not just a square, it's a cube (like an ice cube). This same ability shows us the difference between a circle and a ball. Much of our visual-spatial understanding takes place in the right hemisphere of the brain.

Weaknesses in Visual-Spatial Abilities

Some kids struggle with their visual-spatial abilities. When they are young, many of them have trouble learning left from right. They may have difficulty recognizing or telling the difference between particular letters of the alphabet. They may be delayed in learning how to read. But, if their language skills are good,

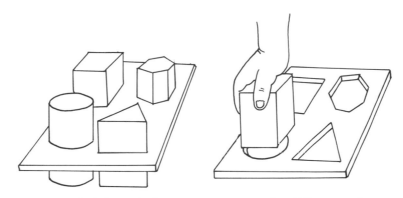

Visual-spatial abilities help us to appreciate the differences between shapes. In the left example above, someone's visual-spatial skills allowed that person to fit the right shapes into the right spaces on the board. On the right side, someone seems to be trying to get a cube into a circular space. Probably he or she has significant visual-spatial problems. (Or, possibly the person is not concentrating.)

they should be able to read pretty well sooner or later. Some students with poor visual-spatial abilities have a hard time with writing and spelling. They have trouble remembering how to make certain letters, and sometimes they spell words the way the words sound rather than the way they should look. For example, a student might spell the word *fight* as *fite*. Some kids with visual-spatial problems do poorly in arithmetic. This is especially true when it comes to picturing things like fractions, triangles and rectangles, or areas and perimeters.

Strengths in Visual-Spatial Abilities

While some kids are weak in their visual-spatial abilities, others are strong. For example, some people are really great at understanding complicated things they see. They may be terrific at fixing a bicycle, figuring out how to build a fort, picturing things in three dimensions, or doing all sorts of arts and crafts activities. As we mentioned in the last chapter, sometimes a student can use her strong visual-spatial abilities to overcome language problems. For example, someone who is having a lot of trouble understanding a teacher's explanation of how to do a math problem might look carefully at a correctly solved problem. This would be especially helpful if the student is mostly a visual learner. Remember, no two kids are exactly alike. A visual-spatial disorder in one kid may cause problems that are different from the problems of another kid with a visual-spatial disorder.

SEQUENCING

Understanding and remembering information that comes into your mind in a particular order is called sequencing ability. As you get older, you can understand and hold longer and longer sequences in your memory. If you give a six- or seven-year-old student a list of numbers to repeat, he or she will probably be able to repeat about four or five of them in the correct order. By age fourteen or fifteen, most kids can repeat six, and some kids can remember seven numbers in the right order.

Sequencing ability is helpful for following complicated directions. Often a teacher will give you several steps to do, and you have to do them in the right order, or you are almost sure to get the wrong answer!

Sequencing ability is also important for understanding how time works. So, it is not surprising that some students who have sequencing problems get mixed up about the days of the week or the months of the year. They keep getting them out of order.

Sometimes these same students are late in learning how to tell time (unless they have a digital clock). When they are very young—before they even go to school—these kids may be mixed up about words like *before* and *after*, *now* and *later*, *yesterday* and *tomorrow*. In kindergarten, they may go up to the teacher and say: "Are we going to have recess before?" and "Did we have it later?" Such quotes show how mixed up they are about time! Some kids show sequencing problems when they get to junior high school. They have trouble arranging their ideas in the right order in a report or essay. They may get confused about the order of their classes at the beginning of the school year, and they may have trouble figuring out how to schedule their time. In other words, students with sequencing problems are often pretty disorganized!

Improving Visual-Spatial and Sequencing Abilities

Kids can be helped to overcome difficulties with sequencing or with their visual-spatial abilities. Teachers can be a big help, but kids can help themselves too. The first thing to do is to recognize the problem. Then, there are specific steps you can take, depending on what kind of a weakness you have. For example, if you have trouble remembering things in the correct order, you should write things down as you hear them. Also, your teacher needs to know that big "chunks" of sequenced material are hard for you to take in all at once. He or she may need to slow down and repeat instructions or explanations so that you can get them registered properly. Sometimes it's useful to whisper under your breath and repeat a sequence as it is being said. This is called *subvocalization*, a technique we mentioned in the chapter on memory. Subvocalization is excellent for registering long sequences. Whether your problem is visual-spatial or sequential, you need to be given a smaller amount of information at a slower speed if you are to understand it.

As usual, you need to use your strengths to strengthen your weaknesses. For example, if you have poor visual-spatial abilities, you might try describing things in words in order to understand and use them. For you, this might be more helpful than trying to picture how certain shapes look in space. In such a case, you might say that a rectangle has four sides and its corners are all right angles.

MOTOR FUNCTION

The third important ability we will discuss in this chapter is motor function. Motor function has to do with our muscles and how well they perform. The word *motor* probably makes you think of an engine or a machine that produces movement. You might think of a motor in a car or in an electric fan. Believe it or not, the human body contains a lot of different motors (muscles). These motors are controlled by your brain. When you use these motors properly, they get stronger and stronger. There are the motors that make your arms and legs and whole body move through space so you can walk to school, play sports, and do chores. There is one big motor called the heart in the upper part of your body. Its job is to keep blood moving through your body. There is another whole system of motors that help you digest your food. There is a set of motors that you use to move your fingers. Any group of motors that work together in your body is called a system.

There are two motor systems that are especially important

to kids in school. One is the gross motor system and the other is the fine motor system, and there are big differences between students' gross and fine motor skills. Motor skills result from cooperation between many parts of your brain, including the parietal lobes, the cerebellum, the basal ganglia, the brain stem, and the spinal cord.

Gross Motor Skills

Gross motor skills have to do with getting your whole body to move just the right way. They can allow you to be good at sports. While some kids are excellent athletes, others are not. These students can hate physical education classes because they keep getting embarrassed in front of other kids; they really don't want anyone to know how clumsy they are. Some students have good motor systems for some sports but not for other sports.

Fine Motor Skills

Fine motor skills have to do with getting your fingers to work accurately and quickly. Things like writing, drawing, sewing, and fixing things by hand require fine motor skill. It becomes more and more important in school as you progress through the grades and are expected to write larger amounts of material. A kid may have a fine motor system that is not so good at steering a pencil around a page. Because of this, his writing will be too slow, too sloppy, or too hard to read. Fine motor problems can be a real nuisance when a student is writing a report or taking a test. Sometimes he will have to work so hard to make things neat enough that he will forget the important ideas he wanted to say!

How the Systems Work

To understand how your gross and fine motor systems work, you need to think about the steps that your brain and body go through to produce a *motor action*. Such an action is one that you perform intentionally. Writing your name, kicking a ball, making a pizza, and tying shoelaces are all examples of motor actions. They are all planned and organized by you for a specific purpose. Tripping and falling, dropping a glass of milk, scratching yourself, or having your leg jerk when the doctor hits your knee with a rubber hammer are not real motor actions. They are not activities you stop to think about and plan. The steps that take place in a motor action are shown on page 116.

Setting a Goal: To carry out a motor action, you need, first of all, to set your motor goal or goals. In other words, you need to know what you want to accomplish. For example, you might decide that you want to catch a ball that is about to be thrown to you.

Getting Input: Once you've decided to catch the ball, you need information to let yourself know how, where, and when to catch it. Such information is called input. You need your eyes to tell you exactly where the ball is in space and how fast it's going. You might also use your memory to recall how you've caught balls in the past. Sometimes language information is involved. A coach or a friend may be shouting at you to let you know that the ball is coming and that you need to back up to watch for it. Some information comes from inside your body. Many different nerves scattered throughout your muscles and joints tell you where your body is at any time. Together with your eyes, those nerves inside your muscles and joints give you body position sense. If you're going to keep moving toward the ball, you have to know where your body is from second to second. You need to know about your changing body positions.

Creating a Motor Plan: While your brain is collecting all the visual, language, memory, and body position information, you need to come up with a motor plan. This will be a kind of map or blueprint of how you will do what you intend to do. The motor plan for catching a ball involves stepping toward the ball, keeping your eyes on the ball, putting your hands close together in front of your body, etc.

Starting the Motor Action: Once you have your information and your plan, you can start the motor action. This means you need to decide what muscles to move, how long to move them, and in what order so that you can complete the motor action. This chain of muscle movements is sometimes called motor coordination.

Self-Monitoring: While you are in the middle of the motor action with all of your muscle movements coordinated, you need to get information on how things are going. Are you on the right track for catching the ball? Are your muscles doing what you originally wanted them to do? (Of course, you need to *remember* what you wanted to do.) You may find that you need to make some adjustments. You may need to change position or use a slightly different group of muscles in a slightly different order. This job of watching what you're doing is called self-monitoring. We discussed self-monitoring in the chapter on attention because it requires concentration. Once you monitor what you're doing, you can adjust your motor action so

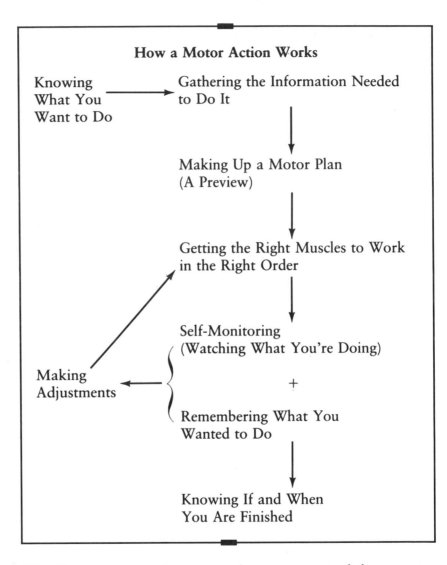

How a Motor Action Works

Knowing What You Want to Do → Gathering the Information Needed to Do It

↓

Making Up a Motor Plan (A Preview)

↓

Getting the Right Muscles to Work in the Right Order

↓

Self-Monitoring (Watching What You're Doing)

+

Remembering What You Wanted to Do

Making Adjustments

↓

Knowing If and When You Are Finished

The diagram above shows you the steps required for a motor action. Once you decide what you want your muscles to do, you have to gather the right information, come up with a plan, get your muscles moving properly, and make ongoing adjustments to smooth out the movements.

that it's just right. Also, you can tell when you're finished, so that you can go on and do something else.

Differences among Students

As you can imagine, some kids are really good in their motor skills, whereas others have problems. Some students have excellent gross motor skills (for things like sports), but they have poor fine motor skills (for things like writing). Some have better fine motor than gross motor skills. It's also possible to be good at some fine motor activities (like drawing) but not at others (like writing). If someone has problems with fine or gross motor function, the chances are that one or more of the steps we have just described doesn't work well. Let's look at some of the possible problems in this area.

Problems

Taking Time To Think: Some kids may have trouble with motor skills because they don't take the time to think about what they're doing when they're involved in motor actions. In Chapter 2, we described some students with attention deficits who tend to be very impulsive. They do too many things too quickly without enough planning or thinking. Sometimes when these students get into a motor action, they go too fast and mess it up. So, students with attention deficits may be clumsy and have trouble with their handwriting.

Using Visual Information: Some kids have difficulty gathering the information they need to make their motor actions work. There are students who have trouble using visual information (information coming in through their eyes) to guide a motor action. Such a kid may have trouble catching a ball because he or she can't quite figure out exactly where objects are in space, where they are headed, and where and when they will arrive in a particular spot. A kid like that who is trying to catch a ball may have trouble deciding when the ball is going to start coming down.

Others have difficulty using visual information to steer their fingers, so they find it hard to copy from a blackboard. Or, it may be hard for someone to draw things accurately because visual information doesn't suggest to his brain a special set of movements with a pencil.

Using Verbal Information: Someone else may have trouble using verbal information or language to guide a motor action. He or she may have serious problems understanding directions from a coach or from an art instructor or dance teacher.

Getting Information from Your Muscles to Your Brain: Some students have trouble writing because their brains do not get accurate reports from their fingers while their fingers are moving. This is called *finger agnosia*. Normally, the nerves of the muscles and joints in our fingers report to our brain and tell us, for example, that our pencil is just about at the bottom of the first stroke of an *h*. Our brain then tells our fingers that it is time to start the final curving stroke of the letter *h*.

Students who have trouble getting information from their fingers to their brains may keep their eyes close to the page because they need to see where in the letter their pencil is. Having to watch so closely can slow them down, and it can also take up too much of their attention (which might mean that their ideas will not be very good).

There are some students who have so much trouble getting information from the small muscles in their fingers to their brains that they actually stop using these muscles. By covering certain fingers with the thumb, a person actually writes more with muscles of the wrists and elbows than with finger muscles! Such a person has an unusual way of holding a pencil. (See the pencil grip in the upper-left corner of the illustration on page 169.)

Some kids have gross motor problems because their brains don't get the information to keep track of where their bodies are! These kids are said to have poor body position sense. They are likely to be a little clumsy and have trouble in sports like skiing and gymnastics that require a lot of balance.

Using Motor Memory: Some people have trouble with motor memory. It is hard for them to learn to do something with their hands or feet and then remember how to do it later. These kinds of motor memory problems might cause someone to have trouble remembering dance steps, remembering how to fix something (the way it was shown to them or the way they did it the last time), or trouble learning how to tie shoelaces.

Writing and Spelling: Motor memory can be a problem especially for writing. There are students who take a very long time to learn how to make letters. Even after they have learned, it is still hard for them to remember how to make letters. They have trouble getting the motor movements for letter formation to be automatic. Some kids in school never really feel good about cursive writing because it's too hard for them to remember all the hundreds of little movements that they need in order to make cursive letters and to connect them in words. When you watch them write, their writing is full of crossing out and false starts.

Kids with motor memory problems have some of the worst handwritings in the world. Many kids with motor memory problems prefer to use printing or manuscript rather than cursive writing. Printing seems to put less strain on their memories. When you print, you have to remember only twenty-six motor patterns (one for each letter). On the other hand, when you write in cursive, every word is a different set of movements to recall.

A lot of students with motor memory problems also have spelling problems. A student, her teachers, and her parents should understand *why* she can't write well or hates to write. At least some of the time it may be because her fine motor memory doesn't work too well.

Getting Muscles To Work Together: There are some people who have poor fine or poor gross *motor coordination*. Somehow, they just can't get all their muscles to work together to cooperate in the right way to accomplish a motor action. This problem has a strange name. It is called a *dyspraxia*. There can be either a gross motor or a fine motor dyspraxia.

A *gross motor dyspraxia* can make it hard to be good at certain sports. A kid might find that he knows what his muscles should do, but they just don't seem able to do it. After watching his coach show the class how to dribble a basketball, one boy with a dyspraxia commented: "I know what he's doing. I could explain how to do it to other kids. It's just that *my* muscles won't do it!"

Students who have *fine motor dyspraxia* are confused about which muscles and fingers to use to make particular letters or words. These students sometimes hold a pencil straight up and down or very tightly and extremely close to its point. This helps them control their muscles better, but it may also make their hands hurt a bit. It can also make writing pretty slow.

Some kids with a fine motor dyspraxia also seem to have an *oral dyspraxia*. They can't get their mouth muscles to work right, so they mispronounce certain words. The parts of the brain (such as areas in the frontal lobes) that control finger movements are located right next to the part that controls the mouth. Therefore, it is not surprising that a weakness in that area of the brain might cause a dyspraxia that affects speech as well as finger movements.

Self-monitoring: Some people coordinate their muscles pretty well but are not too good at self-monitoring. They seem to forget to check on how they are doing while they are accomplishing some motor action. Then they have trouble making the right adjustments in their movements.

Motor Problems and the Brain

In Chapter 1, we described various parts of the motor system of the brain. Students who are having motor difficulties may have some weaknesses in just about any part of the motor system. There may be weak connections in the motor cortex (in the rear of the frontal lobes), in the cerebellum or basal ganglia, or even in the nerves in the spinal cord that go out to the muscles. As we have seen, it is also possible for the brain to have trouble using certain kinds of incoming information (from the eyes, ears, or muscles themselves) to regulate motor movements.

Helping Motor Systems Work Better

Remember, the motor systems in the body are like the motors in cars. When they're not working well, some things can be done to help them work better. For example, a coach can help a kid improve his or her motor skills for sports. Sometimes, someone with poor gross motor skills just needs much more practice than other people to get good at something. In Chapter 6, we will suggest ways to improve motor skills for writing.

Of course, it's a bit harder to fix a kid's motor system than it is to fix a car's engine. For one thing, engines are not usually born with problems. Also, you can't simply order new parts to replace parts that aren't working well in your fine or gross motor systems. It would be wonderful if a teacher could let you know your motor memory was broken so that on your way back from lunch you could stop at the school's brain parts department (near the guidance office) to pick up a new motor memory valve! Even if you could get the right part, no one would know how to install it.

Motor Skills and Success

Everybody needs genuine motor success and praise. Ideally, every kid should have at least one set of motor actions that works really well for him or her. If you want to grow up feeling really good about yourself, you need to be able to show off a few excellent things that your body or your hands can do. You just need to find out what those excellent things are likely to be for you. Sometimes you have to experiment a little.

If you have trouble using visual information to play sports, you will probably find baseball, tennis, and football a bit difficult. You might be better off becoming good at horseback riding, swimming, gymnastics, track, or hiking. These are activities that require motor memory and mostly information that comes from inside your muscles and joints instead of from your eyes. So, by thinking about your own strengths and weaknesses, it is possible to come up with a plan to feel good about some motor performances of your own.

Having some good motor abilities is a great way to get recognized! On the other hand, to grow up being embarrassed about how your body works (or doesn't work) is painful. It can make a kid extremely unhappy. If you have a gross motor problem, you need to understand its causes. Sometimes it is helpful to work with a coach or some other person who understands a lot about motor actions. Such a person can help you reach that exciting goal called motor mastery.

THINKING SKILLS

Thinking is something you do all the time while you are awake. At night, while you sleep, you either dream or you do very little thinking with your brain. Much of the time during the day you are on your own; you can think about whatever you want to. You can think about funny stories, your friends, or neat ideas. You can think about what you want to do next weekend or what you'd like to buy. But, when it comes to school, you often have to think about things that somebody else picks out so that you can learn. This can be a strain on your brain. It is this kind of hard thinking that can be a major problem for some students as they try to succeed in school.

Thinking is a real skill, and like other skills it can always be improved. One important way to improve thinking is to do some thinking about thinking. This can be tricky because to think about thinking you need to think! You get a lot of practice in thinking, but probably you don't often stop to think about your thinking and how it affects your schoolwork. This section of this book is designed to guide some of your thoughts as you start to think about thinking. We will consider four kinds of thinking skills that get used in school: 1) Understanding and Using Concepts, 2) Solving Problems, 3) Forming Ideas, and 4) Thinking Critically.

Understanding and Using Concepts

What Is a Concept?   It's not so easy to understand what's meant by the term *concept*. A concept is something that helps us organize our thinking. It does this by grouping or bringing together facts or ideas that somehow belong with each other.

There are a huge number of concepts and groups of concepts that we use all of the time. For example, if we see a bowl containing grapes, apples, oranges, and cherries, we might call it a "fruit bowl." We call it a fruit bowl because all of the things inside that bowl belong together—they are all part of a concept called fruit. Another example can be found in dogs, cats, parakeets, and guinea pigs. They can all be grouped together as animals, but they also fit our concept of pets. In school, you might learn about the concept of a triangle. Forever after that, every time you see a shape that is made out of three straight lines drawn together, you will think of a triangle. It doesn't matter whether the triangle is large or small, whether it is made out of wood or metal, or whether it is simply lines on a piece of paper. It will still fit the concept of triangle. Another concept is something called "fair play" or "being a good sport." This includes not cheating, following the rules, and being a good loser.

As you grow up, the concepts you need to understand get harder and harder. Fruits and pets are pretty easy concepts. Concepts like fractions, percentages, adjectives, molecules, and atmospheric pressure are much more complicated. As you go on in school, you must keep adding new concepts to your store of knowledge, change some old ones, and even see how some concepts are built out of other concepts. For example, the concept of democracy includes within it concepts like free speech and equality.

Can You Really and Truly Understand Concepts?   In terms of concepts, the big question will always be: How well do you understand old and new concepts? You might be able to repeat (like an echo) what the teacher said to define a concept without really understanding it. Or, you might barely or partly understand it. Or, you might understand it well enough to discuss the concept in your own words rather than the teacher's. You might even be able to explain it to some other student who is having trouble understanding it.

Can You Use Concepts?   If you really understand a concept, you will be able to use it to form new concepts or to solve some problems on your own. For example, one boy, after learning about decimals, discovered how to figure out batting averages on his baseball team.

If you memorize the multiplication tables but only barely understand the concept of multiplication, eventually you may have some real problems in math class. Unless you *truly understand* how multiplying one number by another number works and what is actually happening during that process, then it might be hard for you to teach someone else all about multiplication. It might also be hard for you to use multiplication properly to solve word problems, and you'd probably have a hard time using multiplication in your everyday life. For example, suppose you want to be sure that you have enough money to buy three slices of pizza when you go to the pizzeria. You know that each slice costs $1.25, but you also have to understand the concept of multiplication to figure out how much money you need to take with you. You might also want to add some money for a drink. If you want to buy a drink for your friend, you will need to multiply the drink money by two.

Different Levels of Grasping Concepts

Let's pretend that a math teacher has just described the concept of a fraction in class. The following are some possible levels of understanding of the concept. Each level of understanding in this list is called a grasp.

Level Zero—Unrecognized Poor Grasp
- You don't understand the concept, and you don't realize that you don't understand the concept.
- (You think fractions sound pretty "cinchy," but you don't ask yourself if you really understand them.)

Level One—Recognized Poor Grasp
- You don't understand the concept, but at least you know

that you don't "get it." This means that you should get some help.

- (Fractions don't make any sense to you, and you know you don't understand them.)

Level Two—Partial Grasp

- You understand part of the concept but not all of it. Sometimes you know that you don't have a full grasp.
- (To you, a fraction is a thing with one number on top of another number. That's all you know about fractions.)

Level Three—Remembered Partial Grasp

- You can remember the concept and repeat it pretty much the way the teacher said it, even though you don't fully grasp it.
- (You can repeat the teacher's explanation of fractions, but you don't fully understand them.)

Level Four—A Grasp You Can Teach

- You fully grasp the concept; you can explain it to someone else in your own words; and you can think up your own examples of the concept.
- (You can explain how fractions work to your friend who is a year behind you in school. You might tell him how fractions are used in recipes, with money, and for telling time.)

Level Five—A Grasp You Can Use

- You fully grasp the concept, and you can use or apply it the way that the teacher showed you.
- (You are able to add and subtract fractions the way that the teacher demonstrated in class.)

Level Six—A Grasp You Can Apply Differently

- You fully understand the concept and can think up different ways to apply it.
- (You realize you can use fractions to figure out how to spend your earnings or your allowance.)

Level Seven—A Grasp You Can Use for Original Thinking, Critical Thinking, and Comparing Concepts

- You fully understand the concept, and you can use it to

create new ideas, examine other people's thinking, and compare the concept to other concepts.

- (An example of the last kind of grasp can be found in the study of decimals. If you are just learning the concept of decimals, you might think about how decimals are different from whole numbers and how they are a little like fractions. Deciding how decimals are similar to fractions and how they are different from fractions actually helps you get a stronger grasp on the concept of decimals. You are comparing a concept that is new to you to one that you have learned before; and that comparison improves your grasp of the new concept.)

Verbal and Non-verbal Concepts: You often have two choices when you think about concepts—your mind can think about most concepts either verbally or non-verbally. The word *verbal* has to do with language, which we discussed in Chapter 4. Verbal concepts are concepts that are thought about in words. Politeness is often thought about as a verbal concept. When someone mentions politeness, you group together a whole series of ideas that you can express in words. These include saying "please" and "thank you," not interrupting, and taking turns. Other concepts that are often easy to put into words include friendship, teamwork, motivation, and Communism.

Non-verbal concepts, on the other hand, are concepts that are pictured or visualized rather than put into words. The concept of volume (such as the amount of juice in a bottle) may be easier for many people to picture than to explain in words. Other concepts that are often thought about without language include proportion, ratio, computer byte, and electrical energy.

As you're growing up, it is common to learn about a concept non-verbally before you learn it verbally. For example, a three-year-old child may understand that ants, flies, spiders, and bees "go together" before he has the verbal concept called *insect*.

You might recognize that many of the concepts that are easily visualized or pictured occur in mathematics and science, while a lot of verbal concepts are found in English, social studies, and history. Of course, there *are* concepts in mathematics and science that are easy to put into words, and there are some concepts in social studies that are fairly easy to picture.

Whether a concept becomes verbal or non-verbal depends mostly upon the person who is trying to use or understand it. As you might imagine, some students prefer forming verbal concepts, while others may feel concepts are easier to understand when they are non-verbal. There are some kids who try to get just about all of their concepts into language, while others prefer to create imaginary pictures of concepts whenever they can.

Picturing a Concept and *Putting It into Words:* In school, it is probably important to be good with *both* verbal and non-verbal concepts. It is especially useful to think about a concept by picturing it *and* by putting it into words. Doing this will give you a very strong understanding of the concept; it will also make it easier to remember and use. For example, in a science class it may not be hard to picture a liquid evaporating into the air. You can picture a glass whose water level keeps dropping even though no one has drunk out of it. You might also be able to use words to explain to someone what happens when water stands around for a long time and some of it becomes a gas and escapes into the atmosphere.

Abstract and Concrete Concepts: Some of the most difficult concepts to master are what we call abstract concepts. Abstract concepts usually are those that you cannot see, handle, hear, taste, or smell. The concept of a vegetable is not at all abstract. It is said to be concrete because vegetables are easy to see. On the other hand, concepts like attitude, irregular fractions, human rights, and conservation are more abstract and therefore more difficult to understand. Abstract concepts can even be hard for teachers to teach! They usually take longer to explain.

When kids are very young, almost all of their concepts are concrete. As they go through school, they have to learn more and more abstract concepts. Some students with learning disorders have serious problems understanding certain abstract concepts. The more abstract the concepts become, the more trouble they have. They like concepts they can picture, concepts that are truly concrete, practical, and part of everyday life.

Process Concepts: Other concepts are process concepts. They are used to help explain how things happen or how they work. For example, the concept of multiplication is supposed to make you think about what is actually happening to the numbers involved in the process of multiplying one number by another number. The concept of jet propulsion involves a process that goes on as an airplane flies through the air. To understand the concept of jet propulsion, you need to have a good grasp of the various steps involved in the working of a jet engine. If you don't really understand the steps, you probably have only a slight understanding of the concept of jet propulsion and therefore only a little understanding of how jet planes fly. Thus, just as a concrete concept and an abstract concept each contains a group of characteristics or things that go together, a process concept contains a group of steps that occur to make something happen.

As you're learning a new concept, it is helpful to decide whether

Three Important Kinds of Concepts and Some Examples

Concrete Concepts: Concepts you can see, handle, hear, smell, or taste.

Examples: Mammals
Fast food
Furniture
Antiques
Shopping Malls

Abstract Concepts: Concepts you can use and think about but you can't see, handle, hear, smell or taste.

Examples: Pride
Friendship
Imagination
Infinity
Freedom

Process Concepts: Concepts that help explain how things happen or work. (In order to understand process concepts, you need to understand steps and how they "go together" to make something occur.)

Examples: Digestion (how food gets used by your body)
Photosynthesis (how plants make energy)
Combustion (how things burn)
Long Division (how a long number gets divided by another long number)
Solar Energy (how the sun's rays are converted to electrical power)

the concept includes steps in a process (like long division) or a group of characteristics (like the things insects all have in common). If it is a process, you can strengthen your understanding if you talk about the different steps involved and how they fit together to make something happen. If it is not a process, you may find it helpful to list the different characteristics that go together to make up that concept. You can also say why certain characteristics would not fit that concept.

Really **Understanding Concepts:**   As we have already stated, it is most important *that you really and truly understand the concepts* in a subject you are studying. It is equally important for you to know *whether* you really and truly understand the concepts. Some kids who are having trouble in a subject are doing badly because they only partly understand the concepts. Things get even worse when a student who only partly understands the concepts thinks (or pretends) that he or she fully understands them. Sooner or later this student will run into trouble in that subject.

If you are finding a subject too difficult, you need to identify the important concepts in that subject and consider the possibility that you have no understanding or only a weak or partial understanding of them. You may not understand all the parts of some of the concepts and why or how they fit together to make up that concept. For example, you may hear someone mention electricity. You may then think about wires, plugs, fuses, shocks, and light bulbs, but you may not really understand how electricity works to light up a room. You, therefore, have only a partial grasp of the concept of electricity. Some kids actually fool themselves (and everyone else) into believing they understand something. It is as if they are afraid to test their grasp on concepts because they want so much to believe that they understand them. This is not such a good idea. It's far better to identify the tough concepts, review them, talk about them, draw pictures or diagrams of them, list their parts, try teaching them to someone else, and get help finding as many excellent examples (verbal and non-verbal) or interesting uses for the concepts as you can. If you want, you can practice what we've just suggested by trying to decide if you now understand the concept of a concept!

Solving Problems

We have to solve problems all the time, so the ability to be a good problem solver is an important thinking skill. Outside school, there are social problems, personal problems, health problems, and problems with things that break (such as a bicycle chain). People are very different from each other in their abilities to solve various types of problems. Some people are really good at stopping and thinking and figuring out the best way to solve a problem. Other people just do the first thing that comes into their minds. They may be a bit impulsive. (Remember that word from Chapter 2?) They just don't look around for the best or easiest solutions to problems.

Obviously, problem solving in school is crucial. You come across one problem after another in almost every subject, almost every day. Math problems are the most obvious ones. But there are also problems to solve in figuring out the meaning of a story, deciding what to write in a book report, taking a multiple-choice test, and doing a project for social studies.

To be a good problem solver, you should try to do the following things.

1. **Understand very well what is being asked.** When you are faced with a question or an assignment, you will never do a good job if you do not spend time trying to figure out exactly what is wanted or needed.

2. **Decide what information in the problem or assignment can help you.** You must also decide what information would be of no help at all.

3. **Think of *several* different ways to solve the problem.** It is not good to think about only *one* possible solution or method.

4. **Try to predict what the solution or final product will look like.** If you are solving a mathematics problem, it is a good idea to estimate roughly what the answer will be. If you are multiplying 27 by 10, and your answer comes out less than 10, you should realize that you have made a huge mistake!

5. **Pick your best method and try it.** Think about your several possible methods and decide which one is most likely to succeed.

6. **Think about any knowledge, rule, or skill that you already have that can help you solve the problem.** In other words, you have to look through the drawers in your memory. In a mathematics problem, this may involve remembering the multiplication tables, the steps needed to divide, the way to write certain numbers, or the method to use to find percentages.

7. **Be flexible.** You should be willing to change your mind or give up a particular strategy and use another one if you find that the first one isn't working too well. You need to come up with temporary solutions or ideas and be willing to make

changes. You should keep trying things out. Don't give up and don't feel that the way you started doing something is the only way to do it.

8. **Watch what you are doing.** A good problem solver has to keep getting feedback. You have to check your work. You have to see whether the answer is close to your original estimate. You should keep reviewing what you're writing in things like book reports to see whether you're answering the questions that the teacher asked or whether you're wandering too far off the topic. Remember, all this is part of self-monitoring. It is only with good self-monitoring that you can keep up your flexibility while you solve problems.

Getting Extra Help with Problem Solving: Some students with learning disorders are not very good problem solvers. Either they solve problems too quickly and carelessly, or they are too rigid. They just don't think systematically and flexibly about problems. Sometimes someone needs to work with them to practice good problem solving strategies. These students need help in moving through the steps of problem solving and in developing organized and flexible thinking.

Forming Ideas

Insights: An important part of schoolwork is the ability to come up with your own ideas. One kind of idea is called an insight. An insight is a great thought that comes to you and clears up some confusion or lack of understanding. It may be a sudden understanding of a concept that you never understood before that point. Or, it may be an idea that you get about someone else's ideas. For example, you may be reading a story and suddenly develop your own idea of what the writer of the story wants to communicate.

Original Ideas: Some ideas are called original ideas. These are thoughts that you make up yourself. They give you a chance to be imaginative and creative. There are many students who are great at forming ideas of their own but not so good at understanding other people's ideas. Such students often have interesting and exciting minds, although they may have trouble doing well in school.

It's important to use some of your talents to show your originality. Incidentally, one of the most original products that you can create is yourself. Some students feel that they have to be just like everyone else; however, there is really something to be said for being original. You can be much more interesting if you try to do at least a few things that other kids don't ordinarily do. Of course, the activities you choose should be ones that don't create problems for you or anyone else. Unusual hobbies, collections, or activities during vacations can really set off a kid as interesting and special.

Brainstorming: When you develop ideas, you often brainstorm. Brainstorming involves thinking up original ideas or putting together the ideas of others in your own way in order to explain something, solve a problem, or create a new method of doing things. Brainstorming always takes time; there's no such thing as impulsive brainstorming. Some kids hate to brainstorm. They like to get exact directions from a teacher so that they don't have to think hard to come up with their own ideas for something like a topic for a paper.

Different kids show their brainstorming skills in different ways. These include creating original artwork such as paintings or sculpture, writing things like poems or essays, and building things such as forts or playhouses. Sometimes it is fun to join with another kid and brainstorm together. This is good practice because in the adult world many projects get accomplished through groups of people brainstorming. Together, they think up things like designs for new shopping malls, new laws, and new products.

Some Things That You Can Do by Brainstorming

Think up your own topic and title for a report
Think about what you already know so you can put
    together the right facts to write a report
Produce your own science project
Create your own music or artwork
Invent something
Improve something that already exists
Solve conflicts between people

Important Parts of Brainstorming

Having a goal
Thinking hard about your goal
Taking your time while you're thinking
Letting your mind "run free" so you can think of a lot of
    possible ways of reaching your goal
Selecting your best ideas—figuring out which ones are
    most likely to work
Figuring out how and when to try out your best ideas

Thinking Critically

Another kind of thinking is called critical thinking. When you think critically, you use knowledge as well as your own point of view about something to decide what's right and what's wrong in someone else's ideas. For example, you might read an article in a magazine and decide whether you agree with it. You are thinking critically when you do this because you are coming up with your own opinions and also using any facts you can find to come to conclusions about what's good and what's bad in the article.

Some students are really excellent when it comes to critical thinking. Some may even be too good; they seem to argue about so many things. Such students often feel very negative about almost everything. Just the right amount of critical thinking is important in school. You should not believe everything that you hear or read. Therefore, you need to be able to evaluate ideas to see if they reflect good judgment. If you are using your critical thinking skills well, you can write good book reports, become good at debating or arguing, and get much more out of news-papers, magazines, and even everyday conversations. Below, you will see some of the steps that are important in two different kinds of critical thinking.

Two Kinds of Critical Thinking Skills

Evaluating Other People's Ideas

To evaluate someone else's ideas you should do the following:

- Understand what the other person thinks. This means figuring out what he or she has written or said.
- Separate facts from opinions.

- Decide whether the facts are correct.
- Figure out the person's point of view or opinion in general.
- Decide whether or how much you agree with the opinion.
- Understand why you agree or disagree with the point of view.
- Come up with facts or concepts to try to prove your point of view.
- Put your opinion into your own words.

SOME EXAMPLES

- Listening to a speech by someone who's running for student government
- Reading an article about who's the best football player in the league
- Writing a book report

Evaluating Things

To evaluate a product, you should do the following:

- Decide what something is meant to be or do.
- Figure out whether it does what it's supposed to do.
- List its strengths and weaknesses.
- Decide whether its strengths can overcome its weaknesses.
- Find out if something else can do the job better.
- Come up with an opinion of the product.
- Express your opinion of the product in your own words.

SOME EXAMPLES

- Deciding whether to buy a particular kind of computer or bicycle
- Knowing whether to believe what you see and hear on a television commercial
- Deciding why you like a particular kind of music or art

DIFFERENT STYLES OF THINKING

It is important to realize that no two people think in exactly the same way. In fact, there are many different styles of thinking. A person can be good at thinking in one subject but not so good at thinking in another. For example, a student may be a great problem solver when it comes to fixing something like a cassette player that's not working, but have a hard time with problem solving in mathematics or book reports. Other people are good thinkers in mathematics. Some who are very good at thinking when it comes to moving their bodies through space are often excellent at sports. Still others think well with language. Anything containing many words and sentences helps them to understand concepts, solve problems, form ideas, and think critically. Students who have no trouble at all understanding concepts in sports such as runs batted in or double dribbling may, however, have terrible problems mastering concepts in science or social studies classes. In other words, some brains seem to be specialists at thinking most clearly in certain subjects.

Knowing Your Thinking Strengths and Weaknesses

Every student needs to understand his or her personal thinking abilities and, at the same time, realize that there's no such thing as a completely good thinker or a completely bad thinker. Instead, there are different types of thinkers! With this in mind, you should be aware of subjects, activities, or topics in which you are good at understanding concepts, solving problems, forming ideas, and thinking critically. It is important to know the subjects in which you only partly understand the concepts, the ones in which you are not flexible, the ones in which you are too impulsive in problem solving, and the ones in which you have trouble forming your own ideas. This way you can exercise your good thinking skills inside school, outside school, or both.

Looking to the Future

Knowing your thinking strengths and weaknesses can be helpful for your future too. You can choose a career that uses your strong thinking skills. For example, there are some students who are especially good at thinking about people. They really understand themselves and others. They can brainstorm well about their friends' personal problems. When they grow up, they may pick careers where they can help people solve their personal problems. There are also people who are excellent at musical or artistic thinking. They can become talented artists and musicians. In other words, as we've said before, there are many different kinds of thinking abilities. Some are very handy in school, and some are not too useful in school but are definitely useful elsewhere.

Getting Help

If there is a type of thinking that you don't do well, it is possible to get help. This is especially true if you're weak in the kind of thinking needed for school or for a job. For example, if you are not a very good problem solver, you can be helped to stop and think in an organized way *before* you come up with a strategy or an answer or solution for a problem. The thinking parts of school and of life can be exciting. If thinking in certain school subjects is a problem for you, you need to do something about it by asking for help from teachers, counselors, and parents.

USING YOUR ABILITIES IN SCHOOL

So far in this book we have talked about seven different learning functions. We have discussed attention, memory, language, visual-spatial abilities, sequencing, motor function, and thinking skills. These are some of the important ingredients that allow you to learn and work effectively in school. Let's now try to see how these ingredients are combined as kids learn to read, write, spell, and do arithmetic. By understanding how these functions work together and how they affect each of us differently, it is possible for a student to get some insight into his or her own performance in school. Therefore, in the next chapter we will look carefully at reading, writing, spelling, and mathematics.

The Big Four Skills

INGRID'S STORY

Ingrid is now more than two years behind her classmates in reading. Her trouble first showed up in kindergarten. At that time, her teachers noticed that she could recognize letters but had trouble figuring out the sounds that letters make in words. In first grade, she could look at a word on a page and know that she had seen it before, but she just couldn't remember how to say it. She found it very hard to say the sounds made by combinations of letters. She would see sh *on a page, and her teacher would tell her that those letters make the sound /shhh/. She would say that sound and try to remember that /shhh/ goes with* sh. *But the next day the sound would have vanished from her mind. Her memory couldn't "cement" groups of letters to their sounds.*

As Ingrid went on in school, words kept getting longer, of course. Some had three or four syllables. In order to pronounce a word, she would have to break that word down into its syllables and pronounce each one separately. It was so hard for her to remember how to pronounce each syllable that she could never put all the sounds together to say the word if it had more than two syllables. Ingrid had a reading tutor in school who told her that she had a "decoding problem." This meant that she couldn't break the sound and word code in order to read.

Ingrid loves listening to stories. Fortunately, some of her language abilities are strong enough to allow her to understand stories pretty well when they are read to her. If you give her a paragraph to read, she can understand some of it, even though she has trouble reading it out loud. This is because she can figure out some of the words by knowing what would make sense in the paragraph.

Ingrid gets very frustrated in school. She's embarrassed about her reading problem, and no matter what people tell her, she's convinced that she's dumb. Her older sister and younger brother both do extremely well in school; they find reading very easy. Ingrid's father, however, had the same problem as Ingrid when he was a little boy. This makes her feel a little better because her father is now very successful. He overcame his reading problem, but he still does not like to read very much.

For a long time, Ingrid was getting good grades in mathematics and in any subject that didn't require a lot of reading. But now she is starting to do poorly in all her subjects. Her parents think that she is becoming too discouraged about her reading problems and that this is making her give up. She has become part of a group of close friends who don't do too well in school, and she now feels that they are the most important thing in her life. Little by little, she is losing all of *her interest in school and thinking only about her social life. She just wants to be popular. She feels that she can be successful with other kids but that she can never please anyone when it comes to school work.*

Thinking More about Ingrid

Try answering the following questions about Ingrid after reading all of Chapter 6.

- What problems does Ingrid have when she tries to read?
- Sometimes Ingrid can understand some of what she reads even though she can't read it out loud. What makes her able to do this?
- Why is Ingrid starting to have trouble even in subjects where she doesn't have to read?
- What might happen if Ingrid gets *too* interested in her friends?

GRETTA'S STORY

Gretta doesn't like her math teacher. She says he doesn't explain things well. She also says that he gives hard tests and that he keeps accusing her of not caring about math. Gretta has always found math difficult. She never seems to understand things the first or second time around. She has real trouble understanding fractions and percentages. It seemed to take forever for her to learn long division. Even now, she gets mixed up when she tries to do it. Sometimes, because she doesn't understand explanations, Gretta just tries to memorize what she needs to know. But that doesn't work so well when she's trying to do a word problem or grasp new concepts in class.

When she takes math tests, Gretta panics. There is a little voice inside her that keeps telling her she's going to fail, that she'll never be able to get the problems right. However, Gretta does well in courses where she can use her imagination, where she can be creative. She likes tests where she can give her own kinds of answers, where there's more than one right answer to a question. In mathematics, there is only one answer, and she can't be very creative! That really turns her off.

Gretta's father tries to help her with math at home, but sooner or later they start arguing. Everyone gets frustrated when Gretta tries to do math homework. Sometimes she gets help from a friend. She has also had a tutor in math, but she found the tutorial hours boring and unpleasant. The tutoring didn't help her very much.

Gretta wonders why she has to take math at all. She says she knows she will never use it when she grows up—she will find a career in which she can use her many strengths like reading and writing. She is terrific at expressing herself in words. When she grows up, Gretta wants to be a lawyer. She keeps telling people that lawyers don't have to know any algebra. Gretta's parents keep reminding her that she needs to do well in math to get into college so that she can go to law school and become a lawyer. Gretta hates hearing that.

Recently, Gretta took some tests to find out why she has so much trouble in math. These tests showed that she has difficulty understanding concepts where it is most helpful to picture things, the kinds of concepts that can be hard to put into words. Gretta knows that she has difficulty picturing fractions and really understanding what is going on in a long division problem. The tests also showed that she has trouble recalling math facts quickly and easily. Her weakness in understanding concepts and her memory problems together make math so hard for her.

The people who analyzed Gretta's tests decided that she could be helped by putting mathematics ideas into words, sentences, or rules as often as possible. This encouraged her. Each night she has been going home and trying to describe mathematics concepts in her own words on a tape recorder. As she does this, she pretends that she's teaching the concepts to some younger students. Gretta is using her language strengths to help herself overcome some of her problems in mathematics. This way of learning is definitely helping her. She still wants to be a lawyer, and she now feels more hopeful about achieving this goal.

Thinking More about Gretta

Try answering the following questions about Gretta after reading all of Chapter 6.

- What learning disorders probably cause problems for Gretta in math?
- How is Gretta using her good language skills as a way of improving her math? Do you have other suggestions for her?
- Should Gretta's father keep trying to help Gretta with math at home even though it makes her angry? Is there any way that her father could help her that would not upset Gretta so much?

THE IMPORTANCE OF THE BASIC SKILLS

Reading, spelling, writing, and doing mathematics are often called basic skills. This is because you must be good at them to make it through school. Teachers expect you to show steady growth in these subjects, and by the time you're in high school, your teachers hope that your basic skills are excellent. If they are, you can use them very easily to learn more and more about the world, the universe, the past, the present, and the future.

THE CHALLENGE OF THE BASIC SKILLS

Basic skills are actualy awesome challenges, and some kids find them "slippery." Even though these kids want to learn, the skills they need are hard to grasp, hard to hold on to. Some students have problems with only one basic skill but not the other three. A boy or girl may be a super reader and writer but not so good at mathematics. There are also some kids who are terrific at doing mathematics but who hate to read and can't stand writing reports. Other kids may be very good at many skills needed outside school, but they have real trouble doing well in school because the four basic skills are such a problem for them. Let's now look at reading, spelling, writing, and mathematics and see what it takes to master each of these skills. Then we'll see why some kids have a very hard time with one or more of these basic skills.

READING

The Difference between Reading and Listening

In Chapter 4, we described language as a kind of code created by putting our ideas into words. We saw that the language code is complicated and not easy to learn. When you listen to someone talk, you have to translate all the language sounds into meanings. When you read, you have to translate visual shapes—words and letters—into sounds or meanings or both. That's why reading is so much more complicated than listening. Sometimes, though, reading can bring you different information than you can get simply by listening. For example, think about the title of the book you are now reading. If you simply heard the title, you would most likely think that it would be written *KEEPING AHEAD IN SCHOOL*, but if you look at the cover of this book you will *read* that the title is *KEEPING A HEAD IN SCHOOL*.

Learning To Read

Learning to read takes years of work. Little by little, kids pick up various reading skills. Most kids start out struggling with letters and sounds and end up reading for fun. Let's now look at the different steps involved in learning to read.

The Alphabet

In order to read—or translate the language code when it's put into writing—you must have a good knowledge of the alphabet. You have to be able to identify and say all twenty-six letters

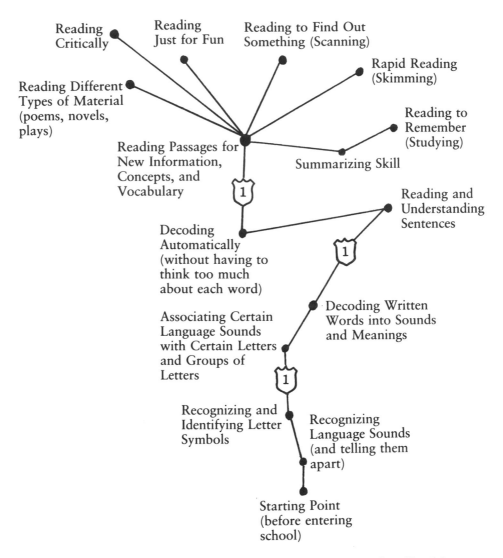

Reading Critically

Reading Just for Fun

Reading to Find Out Something (Scanning)

Rapid Reading (Skimming)

Reading Different Types of Material (poems, novels, plays)

Reading to Remember (Studying)

Reading Passages for New Information, Concepts, and Vocabulary

Summarizing Skill

Reading and Understanding Sentences

Decoding Automatically (without having to think too much about each word)

Decoding Written Words into Sounds and Meanings

Associating Certain Language Sounds with Certain Letters and Groups of Letters

Recognizing and Identifying Letter Symbols

Recognizing Language Sounds (and telling them apart)

Starting Point (before entering school)

The Long Road to Successful Reading: *Learning to read well is like going on a very long trip. You start the voyage before you enter school. You keep improving your reading as you continue your journey (through school and into adult life). This diagram shows the different reading skills you acquire as you travel the "reading road."*

when you see them, and you must see them *correctly*. For example, you have to see the differences between letters that look somewhat alike (like *b* and *d*).

Sound-Symbol Association

After you learn to identify and say the letters of the alphabet, you have to learn the sounds that go with them. For some people this is easy, but for others it is hard. This is because a letter can have a lot of different sounds, depending on what other letters it's combined with. In fact, in some words, a letter ends up having no sound at all. A letter is unsounded either because its sound is "hidden" by the sounds of other letters or because it comes at the end of a word. Some examples of such confusing possibilities are the letter *l* in *balmy* and the letter *e* in *note*.

Learning the sounds that go with particular combinations of letters is called sound-symbol association. Symbols, in this case, are letters. The word *association*, in this case, means that the sounds and symbols "go together." Sound-symbol association is an example of the kind of association we discussed in the chapter on memory, Chapter 3. You have to be able to store all the language sounds that "go with" combinations of letters so that when you see these letters on a page, you'll know how to pronounce them.

As you can see, learning to read requires you to recall many things that can put a tremendous strain on your memory. What's more, your memory and your language ability have to cooperate as you struggle to become a good reader. This causes huge problems for some kids. Many of these kids have great difficulty with sound-symbol associations. Somehow, their brains seem to have no "drawers" for groups of letters that go with sounds.

(We talked about storing things in memory drawers in Chapter 3.) A student may, for example, have an amazing ability when it comes to giving the names of different kinds of cars when she sees them or foods when she smells them, but she won't be able to give the sounds of groups of letters when she sees them. Her memory for *that* association is a problem for her.

Taking Words Apart and Rebuilding Them

Once you can attach sounds to the right letter symbols or groups of letters, you can take written words apart and rebuild them. To rebuild a word, you pronounce each sound separately and then you put the sounds together. This involves figuring out the first sound in the word, then figuring out the second sound in the word, then figuring out the third sound in the word, and so on. While you are working on the third sound, you have to remember what the first sound was, or you'll never be able to get all the sounds together to form a word. All this takes a good active working memory. (We talked about active working memory in Chapter 3.) Once you have formed a word, you check with your word memory to make sure it's a real word. If it comes out sounding like nonsense, then you have to sound it out again. You also have to consider the possibility that you may be encountering a word you've never seen or heard of before!

Decoding and Using Sight Vocabulary

Solving the word code written on paper is called decoding. As you get good at decoding, you don't have to stop and figure out every sound in every word. That would be too slow and much too boring. Little by little, you can build up your sight vocabulary, which is made up of words that you can recognize automatically the instant that you see them. When you have a big sight vocabulary, you start reading faster.

Oral and Silent Reading

Even before you become an instant word decoder with a good sight vocabulary, teachers start having you read sentences, paragraphs, and whole stories, either out loud (orally) or to yourself (silently). When you read out loud, you have to decode every single word to produce the right language sounds. As you go through the lower grades in school, teachers expect you to read aloud more, and to do this more smoothly, easily, and expressively. When some kids with reading problems read aloud, they sound as if they are reading a list of unconnected words. This is called "word-by-word" reading. It's not smooth or easy to listen to. For silent reading, you don't have to be as careful about the sounds in words. When you get good at silent reading, you can see a word on a page and know what it means without ever having to pronounce it. But sometimes, especially when you need to read very slowly and carefully, you might intentionally whisper under your breath while you are reading. This slows you down, helps you concentrate, and makes you pay attention to the individual words.

Reading Sentences and Paragraphs

Reading sentences and paragraphs has some real advantages. One advantage is that when you meet new words in sentences and paragraphs, you have a lot of excellent clues about what those words are. If there's a word that you've never seen before, or even a word that you've never heard of before, you can figure out what it is by deciding what word makes sense in the sentence or paragraph. Take the following sentence, for example: *The squirrel ran away and climbed up on a branch of the guragium.* You do not know what the word *guragium* is. You've never seen or heard of it before. (In fact, *guragium* isn't a real word, but let's pretend it is.) By studying the sentence, you can tell that *guragium* must be some kind of tree. If you were to see that word all by itself in a list of words, you could never figure out its meaning. The process you have just used to figure out the meaning of a new word is called *using context clues*. Some kids are much better at using context clues than they are at decoding individual words.

Another excellent thing about reading sentences and paragraphs is that you can use the information you already have to help you understand new material. If you know about horses, for example, and you read a story about a particular horse, you can get a lot more out of the story because you have had so much experience with horses. In fact, one of the best ways of improving your reading skills is by reading material about which you already know a lot.

Reading Comprehension

Understanding sentences and paragraphs is called reading comprehension, which is not always an easy skill to acquire. Although you can use *context clues* to help in understanding sentences and paragraphs, you really need to be good at *decoding* words too. You need good *language abilities*, including a decent *vocabulary*. Also, you have to understand how sentences work; that is, you have to know something about *grammar* and about how the order of words in a sentence tells you its meaning. The order of words in a sentence is called *syntax* (something we talked about in Chapter 4).

Reading comprehension also requires some other abilities. One is *applying what you know to what you are reading*. When you do this, it is important to remember and apply the right things. You have to know just what facts, ideas, or experiences to pull out of your memory. Sometimes you can do this in advance. For example, if you're reading about airplanes, while you're opening the book you begin to think "airplane thoughts." As you do this, you are opening up a memory drawer in your mind. Then, as you read, you find some things you already know, and also, we hope, some new and useful information that you can fit into one of your memory drawers.

Sometimes, you will not be sure of what information you will need to bring with you when you read. For example, if you take a reading comprehension test in school, you won't know ahead of time what the paragraphs are going to be about. In such a case, as you read each paragraph, you should start to look for certain ideas that remind you of things you already know. Comparing what you read to facts or concepts you already know does more than improve your reading comprehension. It also makes reading much more interesting for you.

Reading comprehension also requires finding out what is most important in the material. This involves *finding a main idea* and then *seeing how other ideas or details give you more information* about the main idea. Sometimes, there are ideas in a paragraph that you can't see or read. Finding ideas like these—ones that are only hinted at but not stated—is called *inference drawing*. (We discussed this in our chapter on language.) As you progress through school, good reading requires a lot of inference drawing.

There are still other abilities that are important for reading comprehension. These abilities include *understanding the concepts; being able to tell how a paragraph, chapter, or book is organized; knowing when to read fast, when to skim, and when to read extra slowly to find some specific fact you need; and being able to figure out the writer's point of view or opinion.* As you go on in school, you have to be able to read many different kinds of material: poems, plays, novels, history books, science texts, newspapers, and so on. For each of these, you need to be able to switch reading gears—to change your speed and style of reading to ensure comprehension.

Remembering What You Read

The ability to remember and then use what you read is often necessary in school. While you're reading, you have to keep remembering what you're reading so that you can hold together many facts and ideas contained in the pages. For some students, this is a big problem. They keep forgetting what they're reading while they're reading it. This means that important information keeps leaking out of their minds.

Often you must remember what you've read for some time after you've stopped reading. Since it is usually impossible to remember every single word from a paragraph or story, you must become very good at remembering and then *summarizing*. To summarize what you read, you have to pick out what's really important and then describe it in your own words. Summarization skills are important for writing book reports, for example. Some kids have tremendous problems with their summarization skills. Sometimes this is because they can't decide what's really important. Or, they have trouble organizing the ideas in the correct order. Some students with language problems have trouble summarizing because they have trouble translating the ideas of a book into their own words, sentences, and paragraphs.

Remembering what you read is crucial *for using what you have read*. Following written directions, participating in class discussions about a book, and using a computer manual are all examples of being able to read, remember, and then do something that you could not have done before. Acquiring this ability is, of course, one of the major reasons that we learn to read.

Reading for Pleasure

Students who find reading pretty easy are the ones who are most likely to enjoy it. They read a lot just for the fun of it. They read outside school; they read books, magazines, or newspapers that no teacher assigns. They often read things that are especially interesting to them. For example, someone who enjoys music may love to read books about singers or songwriters. Someone who loves sports may enjoy reading biographies of athletes.

Since good readers read more than poor readers, good readers get a lot more practice reading. This means that they get better and better at it. On the other hand, most students who find reading hard *never* read for fun. They read only when forced to (usually as part of a school assignment). So, poor readers get less reading practice, and then they become even poorer readers than their classmates. Since reading is a major way to develop language abilities and knowledge, kids who hardly ever read may fall behind in areas other than reading skills. They may not keep up in language abilities and end up knowing a lot less than their classmates. Somehow, poor readers need to start reading for fun. But, reading for them isn't fun; often it's boring. These students need to try to find some subjects or ideas to read about that might interest them. Then, they too can get practice. Poor readers can learn to read well; it just takes them longer, so they need a lot of patience and practice.

Reading Problems

Since so many different abilities are needed for reading, there can be many reasons why a person might not read well. These reasons are stated in the list called "Kinds of Reading Problems" shown on page 159. A reading problem changes as a student gets older. The problem might start out as a decoding problem, and then become a comprehension problem, and then a summarizing problem. So everyone involved in helping the student needs to keep watching closely as the student grows up.

Getting Help for Reading Problems

A student with a reading problem can be helped if the student and his or her teachers and parents understand the reading problem very well. Kids with reading problems are lucky that there are some very fine teachers who specialize in helping kids read. Remedial reading or tutoring can be great. There are all kinds of special techniques for helping kids read better. The trick is to find the right technique for each student. This will depend on the student's learning disorder; it could be problems with memory, with language, with visual-spatial ability, with attention, or with some other part of reading. A reading method can be chosen and fit to a student just as if he or she were

Kinds of Reading Problems

TROUBLE Appreciating Language Sounds
Language sounds don't seem very clear.

TROUBLE Remembering Sound-Symbol Associations
The sounds of combinations of letters are hard to remember.

TROUBLE Holding Together the Sounds in a Word
The sounds of letters are known, but it's hard to put together the sounds in the right order to make words during reading.

TROUBLE Reading Fast Enough
It takes too long to pronounce or understand each word.

TROUBLE Understanding Sentences
The vocabulary or grammar is too hard.

TROUBLE Understanding Paragraphs or Passages
It's hard to find the main ideas and the important details, or it's hard to understand the concepts, ideas, or facts.

TROUBLE Remembering While Reading
Ideas don't stay in memory during reading.

TROUBLE Summarizing What Was Read
It's too hard to decide and remember what's important and to organize important ideas in your own words and sentences.

TROUBLE Applying What Was Read
It's difficult to use what you've read.

TROUBLE Enjoying Reading
Reading is too much work; it's not automatic.

getting a new pair of shoes. Having a reading problem can be embarrassing and discouraging, but there are worse things to have. Most students, if they don't give up, will come out being able to read. The struggle is definitely worth it!

SPELLING

Spelling and Reading—Similarities and Differences

In some ways, spelling is very much like reading. In spelling, just as in reading, you have to attach language sounds to particular combinations of letters that stand for those sounds. But spelling a word is the opposite of reading it: when you read a word, you see its spelling and have to find the sounds to say; when you spell a word, you know the sounds (or you think of the sounds) and you have to remember the letters that make the sounds in that word.

Spelling Problems

Some words are called *regular*. That means if you have a good sense of sound-symbol association, you can figure out their spellings. Other words are *irregular*, or unpredictable. These words may not be spelled the way they sound, or there may be more than one possible spelling for each. You just have to know how to spell words like these. Your memory has to work hard. Examples of spelling words that you just have to remember are shown on page 161. Another problem for spellers is the fact that in some words letters are silent; that is, they never get pronounced. There are also words that have a confusing sound in

---

Some Spelling Words You Just Have To Remember

Correct Spelling	*Common Mistake(s)*
Sword	Sord, Sored
Plumber	Plummer
Ocean	Oshun, Oshin
Rough	Ruff
Weight	Wayt, Wate
Necessary	Nesessery, Nessery
Calendar	Calander
Allow	Alow, Ellow
Sweat	Swet, Swett

---

them because different letters may be able to make this sound. For example, take the word *industry*. If you substitute an *e*, an *i*, an *o*, or an *a* for the *u* in the middle of the word, the word could still be pronounced the same way. There are many other words like that in English. Sometimes you can figure out how to spell them by thinking of words that are very similar to them. For example, for *industry* you could think of *industrial*, which sounds as if it can have only a *u* in the middle. As we've said before, often you just have to use your memory when it comes to confusing words or parts of words. Of course, that means that some students with certain kinds of memory problems won't be impressing their teachers with their spelling abilities!

Here are some common kinds of spelling problems:

• **Problem Number One: Letters and Sounds.** Some students find it hard to remember that a certain combination of letters stands for a certain language sound. Sometimes these students don't have a very good sense of those sounds in the first place.

Their brains may not understand how sounds are different from each other, and they may not be able to register the sounds clearly enough. They often have decoding problems when they read. Some students who can't remember which sounds go with which letters try to picture whole words instead of sounding them out. Because they cannot attach the sounds to the right letters, they still make mistakes. Often their incorrect spellings *look like* good spellings, but their spellings can never be pronounced right. So, such a student might spell the word *brought* as *bruogt*. It looks like the real word, but it certainly can't be pronounced like the real word! Try it!

- **Problem Number Two: Picturing Words.** There are some students who are the opposite of the ones just described. They are pretty good at sounding out words and remembering which letters go with which sounds, but they have trouble picturing words. They can't remember how words look. When they spell, their mistakes often sound good, but what they write doesn't look at all like the real word. These students might spell the word *brought* as *brawt*. When you pronounce the word *brawt*, it sounds right, but it doesn't look much like the real word.

- **Problem Number Three: Spelling Rules.** Some students make mistakes that show a poor understanding of what is allowed in their own language. They may spell words using combinations of letters that don't even exist anywhere in English. They may also have difficulty remembering or using rules for spelling. For example, there is something called the long-vowel rule. This rule says that if there is a vowel followed by a consonant, and if you want to use the long rather than the short pronunciation of that vowel, you have to add an *e* after the consonant. That helps us tell the difference between *bit* and *bite*. The word *bite* has a vowel at the end, so we pronounce the *i* in the long form. *Bit* has no vowel at the end, so it rhymes with *it*. Some students who don't have any appreciation of that rule leave off the final *e*. They might spell the word *create* as *creat* and the word *cute* as *cut*. Often a student who has trouble with spelling rules also disobeys rules in other subjects like mathematics, grammar, and science.

• **Problem Number Four: Inconsistent Spelling.** Some students spell well sometimes but not other times. Often these are kids who have attention deficits. They have real trouble concentrating on little details, and it shows up in their spelling.

• **Problem Number Five: Writing and Spelling at the Same Time.** Some students who can spell individual words, and may even be good in a spelling bee, misspell the same words when they have to write them in a paragraph. Sometimes their teachers and parents think that they are careless or that they're not really trying, and that's why they misspell words they seem to know. Yet, there are some kids who find writing so difficult that they can't write and spell at the same time. We will talk about writing problems in the next section of this chapter. For now, remember that if a student has to work very hard to remember how to make letters, use good grammar, and organize his ideas when writing a report, he may be so busy doing these things that he will forget how to spell some words. In other words, spelling can get crowded out of his memory by all the other things he has to remember while he writes.

• **Problem Number Six: Mixed Spelling Problems.** There are kids who make all different kinds of spelling errors. They may have trouble with the word sounds, the rules, and the visual pictures of words. Kids with these mixed spelling errors seem to have the most trouble improving their spelling.

- **Problem Number Seven: Poorly-Automatized Spelling.** As you get older, you must spell quickly and automatically, as well as correctly. You need to be able to spell easily when you're writing stories or reports. You want to use as much of your attention as possible for ideas. So, a big problem for some students is that they have not yet automatized spelling. It just doesn't arrive fast and easily during writing.

Ways To Improve Spelling Skills

There are many ways to improve spelling. Often tutors and other teachers can suggest some clever techniques to improve a student's spelling. Students can help themselves, too. Reading a lot can help; so can writing. Some students use flash cards or try to make up games. There is also some good computer software to help a student study spelling. When all else fails, there is always spelling software that corrects spelling when used on a word processor. Even if a student uses such software, she should still try to improve her own spelling ability.

Obviously, the main reason you need to know how to spell is so that you can write. So, this is a good time for us to consider writing and writing problems.

WRITING

The Challenge of Writing

Every single function and kind of skill that we have talked about so far is part of the act of writing. Writing combines fine motor function, language, memory, attention, thinking skills, sequencing, and visual-spatial abilities. Not only that, but when we write, we often have to use all of these abilities at the same time! No wonder writing is so hard for so many students, especially those who have learning disorders.

As you advance through your school years, writing demands become more challenging. You have to write longer and longer assignments and take longer and longer tests. As you do this, you have to remember, understand, and obey all kinds of writing rules in the areas of punctuation, capitalization, spelling, and grammar. You have to be able to plan what you are going to write, write it, look back and find mistakes, correct your mistakes, improve what you've written, and make sure that other people can read and understand it. (You also need to be sure *you* can read it!) On a test, you may not have much time to write. This same thing is true when you're taking notes in class. You have to write fast enough to keep up with the flow of ideas.

Negative Feelings about Writing

If you're working on an assignment at home and it's too hard for you to get your ideas down on paper, you may come to feel that writing is boring and tiring. Then you start hating to write, and you write as little as possible. You may even find yourself "forgetting" to hand in assignments. Or you may find writing to be such a pain that you rush through writing assignments as quickly as possible. Nobody likes to take a long time planning and thinking about something he or she doesn't like doing. If you feel this way, you probably don't make corrections, and you probably don't try to improve or polish what you've written. Your teachers or parents might think you're "careless" or that you don't care about the quality of your work. They may not always understand how unpleasant and difficult writing is for you. They may not realize that you dislike writing so much that you feel like writing fast just to get it over with.

A Positive Look at Writing

Believe it or not, writing can be exciting. Many students with learning disorders have excellent imaginations that create original ideas. They may have some trouble putting these thoughts on paper, but once they're down on a page, the student has a great way of holding onto his or her best ideas. Writing is also a way of exploring personal ideas, working things out for yourself. Someone once said: "How can I know what I think until I see what I say?" Words and sentences on paper can't escape (unless you lose your report or use disappearing ink!). So, writing also takes some strain off your memory so that you can think up more great thoughts connected with the ones you have written down. This process is called developing your ideas. All of this means that if you have good ideas, writing is worth the struggle.

Dealing with Handwriting Problems

Dealing with handwriting problems is often part of the struggle. If you have a bad handwriting, it's embarrassing to have other kids correct your papers or read what you've written. Teachers may have to discuss your handwriting with you if it's bad. Most teachers will not deliberately say things to embarrass you in front of other students. So, if talking about your handwriting in class embarrasses you, you can talk to your teacher after class and ask him or her to discuss your handwriting with you only in private. If that doesn't work, you might want to discuss the matter with your parents.

Kinds of Writing Problems

There are many different kinds of writing problems. For now, we will talk about five of the most common ones. A student may have one of these troubles, two of these troubles, or even all of these troubles with writing. Knowing which trouble or troubles you have can help you improve your writing.

- **Trouble Number One: Fine Motor Problems.** Perhaps you remember that we discussed fine motor problems in Chapter 5. There are four common kinds of fine motor problems that can interfere with writing.
  1. Some students have *trouble keeping track of just where their pencil is while they write (finger agnosia)*.
  2. Other students have a *dyspraxia*, a fine motor problem that has to do with muscle coordination. Remember, some kids' brains have trouble deciding exactly which muscles in their fingers need to be pushed and pulled, and in which order, to make the right letters and words. Although they

can picture how letters and words should look, they have a *problem with getting the right muscles to work together quickly and easily.*

3. Another kind of fine motor problem has to do with *fine motor memory.* Students with this problem have *trouble getting finger muscles in touch with memory through many different nerve connections between the hand and the brain.* Motor memory reminds someone how to tie shoe laces, how to play a sport, how to make a bed, and how to form letters and words. Some kids have a motor memory problem that seems to cause their hand muscles to get unplugged from their brains.

4. Finally, some students have problems with *eye-hand coordination.* This means that they seem to have *trouble getting their eyes and fingers to work together.* They may have difficulty learning to tie their shoe laces, fix things, and do various crafts. Sometimes poor eye-hand coordination also makes writing slow and sloppy.

Remember, it is possible to have a fine motor problem that affects writing without causing trouble in other motor activities. Someone with a weak motor memory may still be a terrific artist or a real pro at fixing things. It is possible to have trouble getting feedback from your fingers and still be good at drawing and painting, because, in these activities, you can use your eyes to get feedback.

- **Trouble Number Two: Remembering and Writing at the Same Time.** Writing causes your memory to work very hard. In other chapters of this book, we said that while writing a report, you have to remember punctuation, spelling, capitalization, grammar, vocabulary, letter formation, your own ideas,

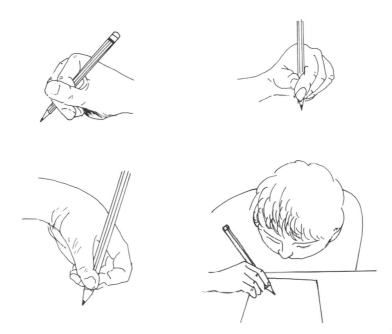

Very often students with fine-motor problems have an awkward way of holding a pencil or pen. In the upper-left corner, you can see the hand of a student who keeps his thumb over his next two fingers as he writes. The small joints in his fingers cannot really move very much; therefore, a lot of his writing takes place with his wrist or big knuckles. Even his elbow may move during writing. In the upper-right corner, a student's hand holds the pencil very close to the point, straight up and down, and extremely tightly.

On the bottom left is the hand of a student bent inward like a hook. This stretches out some of the muscles on the back of the hand, which seems to help certain kids control the pencil. In the lower-right corner is a student who has trouble keeping track of where the pencil is during writing, so he keeps his eyes very close to the page. Since he really has to concentrate on the location of the pencil point, he finds it difficult to remember spelling, good ideas, and other parts of writing.

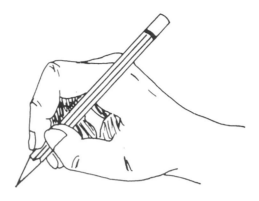

This is an illustration of what is called a normal tripod pencil grip. In this particular grip, the muscles in the thumb and the middle finger are responsible for most of the pencil movement and letter formation. The second finger "goes along for the ride" and controls the pressure of the pencil on the paper. The pencil is held about three quarters of an inch from the point, and the upper part of the pencil is resting near or up against a knuckle. The pencil is held at about a forty-five degree angle with the page. This is probably the most comfortable and efficient pencil grip for most people. However, some kids have trouble writing with a tripod grip. It is worth trying to use this grip, although it may not work out for some kids.

and what the assignment is. That's a lot to remember all at the same time. Not only do you have to remember all of these things at once, but as we have said, you have to remember them quickly. (If you take too long to remember how to make an *h*, you may forget what you want to write.) Students who have trouble with all this can benefit by thinking about an old saying: "If you're trying to learn how to juggle, and you're having trouble juggling with five balls, you'd be better off trying to juggle with four balls. Otherwise, you'll never become a juggler."

It's the same way with writing. If it's too hard to remember all of the different parts of writing all at the same time, you and your teacher need to decrease memory requirements for you, at least temporarily. Your teacher may need to allow you to hand in a report without good spelling as long as the ideas, the punctuation, and the grammar are good. Maybe

Writing—the Awesome Juggling Act: *When you write, you have to remember many things at the same time. In a way, writing is like juggling. In the picture above, the boy is trying to juggle the most important parts of writing. To juggle, he has to keep all of these balls in the air at the same time, just as to write well, you have to keep all of the parts of writing in your memory while you are writing.*

after that, you could do one with great spelling but not such good punctuation. Students who have trouble remembering and writing at the same time also should remember another technique. This technique is called *writing in stages*. The stages include a thinking stage, an idea writing stage, a spelling/punctuation/capitalization stage, and a neatness stage. It's best if each stage is done on a different day so that you don't use too much of your attention at one time.

- **Trouble Number Three: Thinking about Ideas and Writing at the Same Time.** Many students have to work so hard at writing that they just can't think about the ideas they want to express at the same time that they are writing. The huge memory strain that we just described in Trouble Number Two, combined with all the work that your fingers have to do, may take up so much of your brain's energy that the process is too slow, and there is little or nothing left over for thinking up interesting ideas. When this happens, your ideas look silly or simple on paper compared to the ideas that you talk about in class discussion or think about in your head. One boy said, "You know, I can think fast if I don't write, and I can write fast if I don't think. I just can't write fast and think fast at the same time." There are some students who need to separate thinking about ideas from writing. Sometimes it is smart for these kids to dictate their best ideas into a tape recorder, then listen to them, then jot some of them down, and *then* write a report using the stages we discussed in Trouble Number Two.

- **Trouble Number Four: Planning and Organizing.** One reason that writing is so important is that it forces you to organize your ideas so that they can be well understood by other people and by yourself. Even if no one ever reads what you write, your writing can help you arrange your thoughts in a way that makes them more sensible and easier to use and to tell others about. Some kids have severe problems organizing their ideas.

Below is a list of things kids may have trouble with when they write.

1. *Choosing a Topic.* Thinking up something to write about or understanding what the teacher expects.

2. *Deciding Who Will Read the Writing.* Writing so that the reader can understand and like what's written. For example, a writer would use a different style and content for a teacher, a grandmother, a cousin in first grade, or a best friend.

3. *Brainstorming.* Thinking up many good ideas and writing them down.

4. *Grouping Ideas.* Taking all the ideas and putting together the ones that belong together.

5. *Figuring Out the Order.* Knowing what ideas to put first, what ones to put second, etc.

6. *Throwing Out Ideas.* Getting rid of ideas that don't fit, even though they seemed to at first.

7. *Going Back Over What's Been Written.* Making sure that things make sense, that the ideas are organized in the right order.

8. *Changing the Order.* Reorganizing what's been written if necessary.

Many students with writing problems don't seem to know what they are going to write until they write it. Instead of coming up with a plan and sticking to it, they just start writing. Each sentence makes them think of something else to write. They try to write everything as they think of it. They keep changing the subject, even though they don't mean to. As they go on, they get further and further away from the topic they were supposed to write about. For an example of this kind of writing, see Writing Sample D on page 177.

- **Trouble Number Five: Knowing How To Translate Ideas into Language on Paper.** Some students just can't seem to get their ideas into good language. Many times these are students who have trouble expressing themselves or putting their ideas into words even in a class discussion. Some of them find it even harder to do this on paper. Their writing may make it look as if they don't know grammar very well. Their sentences may be short and the vocabulary too simple for their age and grade in school. Language disorders often interfere with writing, since written language is the most complicated kind of language. On the other hand, writing has a good side to it for students with learning disorders. It gives them more time to express themselves than they have when they are called on in class.

Writing Samples

Sometimes just by looking at samples of a student's writing, you can tell a lot about his or her learning disorders. The writing samples on pages 176 and 177 are those of real students.

Sample *A* is the work of a seventh grader who has a fine

motor dyspraxia and some motor memory problems. These difficulties make it very hard for him to form letters quickly and automatically. In long words, he often leaves out important syllables because his memory cannot hold big "chunks" of information during writing. He also has trouble picturing the letters and words in his mind before he forms them. Because his memory for letter forms is a bit weak, he may make the same letter many different ways in a paragraph.

Also, this student prefers printing (manuscript) to cursive writing because in cursive writing he has to remember more complicated motor movements, while in printing he needs to recall only twenty-six patterns of motor movement (one for each letter of alphabet). Incidentally, the student who wrote the paragraph shown in Sample *A* does extremely well in reading. He also has excellent language skills and expresses himself with good ideas when he participates in a class discussion. This is hard to believe when you look at his writing sample, but writing is so difficult for him that he has trouble thinking and expressing himself at the same time he is writing.

Sample *B* is written by an eighth grader who has fine motor problems that make it difficult to write quickly and easily. This student has trouble with a dyspraxia that makes it hard for him to get his finger muscles to move quickly enough. He, too, is a very good reader with a lot of good ideas. But when he writes, his ideas are not so good because writing itself is so difficult. His parents, and sometimes his teachers, think he doesn't really try very hard. He does try, but he often gets discouraged about writing.

Sample *C* is very legible. It was written by a girl who has very good fine motor skills. However, she has a language disorder. You can see that she has tried to fit too many ideas into

Sample A

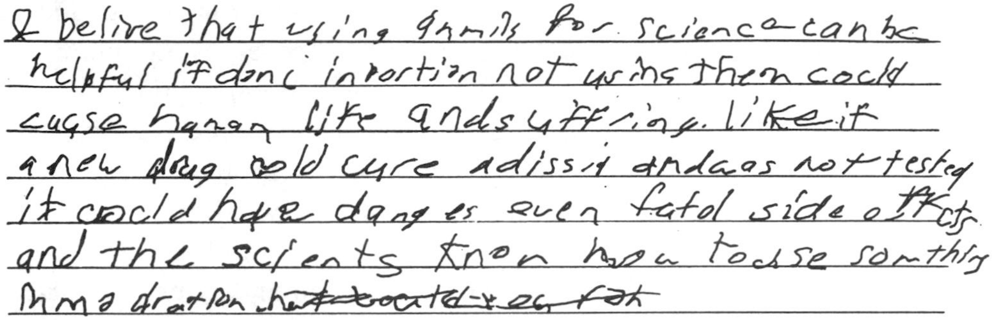

[handwritten text]

I believe that using animals for science can be helpful if done in portion not using them could cause human life and suffering. like if a new drug could cure aids and was not tested it could have dangerous even fatal side effects and the scientists know how to use something in moderation.

Sample B

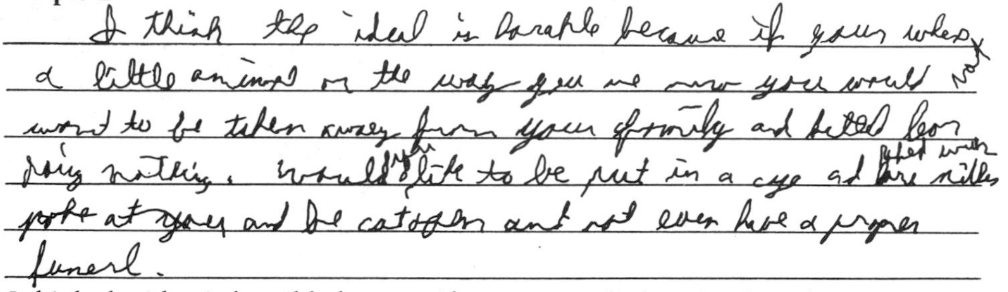

[handwritten text]

I think the idea is horrible because if you were a little animal or the way you are now you would not want to be taken away from your family and killed for doing nothing. Would you like to be put in a cage and poked with needles at you and be cut open and not even have a proper funeral.

Sample C

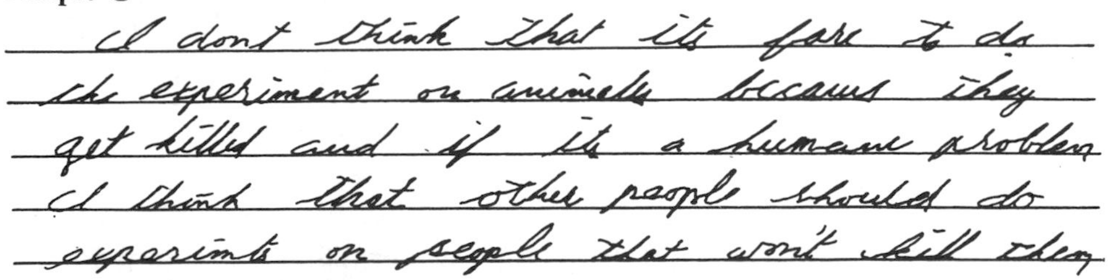

[handwritten text]

I don't think that it's fair to do the experiment on animals because they get killed and if it's a human problem I think that other people should do experiments on people that won't kill them.

Sample D

If I were the principal of this school, I would abolish report cards. Kids might not work hard without grades. Their parents get angry if their grades are too low. Parents shouldn't interfere so much. Kids need to learn to work on their own and you need free time. It's healthy to get outside and play in the fresh air.

Sample E

If I were the principal of this school, there are four things I would do: First, I would stop giving report cards. Instead, I would have teachers just write letters telling you how you're doing. Second, I would ask some student leaders for advice in running the school. Third, I would have classes in music, art, and woodworking, and things like that so kids could all be creative. Fourth, I'd give myself a raise in pay for which I would work harder. Those four things would make this a better school with me as the principal.

RSM

one sentence. Although she has some great ideas, she does not state them very well.

Sample *D* was written by a student who has good language skills and good motor function. There are complete sentences with good vocabulary and perfect spelling. However, the paragraph is disorganized. Instead of having an overall idea that is developed in the paragraph, each sentence seems to lead to a new idea in the next sentence. The student starts out talking about what he would do if he were the principal, and he ends up discussing how important it is to go outside and play. What does that have to do with being a principal of a school?

Sample *E* is an excellent paragraph. It is well written, well organized, and legible. It starts out with a topic sentence and ends up with a concluding sentence. You can tell that this student is a good writer.

Understanding and Helping a Student with a Writing Problem

Students with writing problems can have a very hard time as they go through school. For some reason, grown-ups may be more understanding of students who have reading problems than they are of students who have writing problems. Maybe this is because writing problems often make a student look as if he or she is not really trying. So it is important that everyone—the student, the parents, and the teacher—understands that there is a writing problem that really makes it hard for someone to do reports, copy from the board, take notes or complete written tests. Once the problem is understood, a lot can be done about it.

Below is a list of just a few things that may help students with writing problems.

1. Fixing a poor pencil grip (very gradually).

2. Writing reports in stages in order to deal separately with punctuation, grammar, spelling, capitalization, ideas, etc.

3. Using a typewriter or word processor.

4. Being given more time on tests.

5. Being allowed to write shorter reports.

6. Not having other kids correct their papers.

7. Trying out different kinds of pencils or pens to find the ones that feel most comfortable.

8. Learning how to brainstorm and organize ideas before writing.

9. Learning about different methods of proofreading and revising.

10. Writing about subjects that are familiar, interesting, or fun.

11. Not writing too much at once; for example, writing small amounts each evening and proofreading something *a few days after* you write it.

Writing Skills and Your Future

Most jobs do not require the writing of essays and reports. On the other hand, many require some kind of writing. Besides, as we said earlier, writing is important because it teaches you how

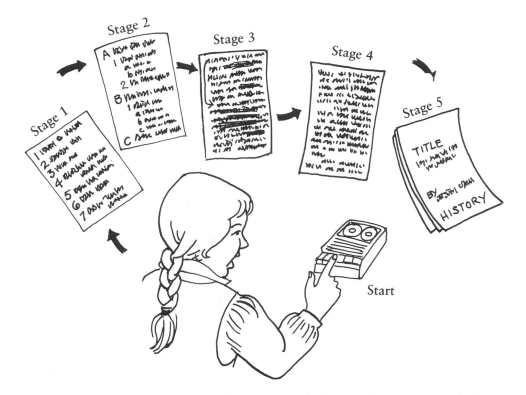

Writing is best done in stages. This is particularly true for students who have writing problems. Many of these students have difficulty thinking and writing at the same time, so sometimes it is good for them to separate thinking from writing. For example, such a student might first dictate her best ideas into a tape recorder. Then, as the first stage in writing, she could listen to the tape recorder and make a list of her best ideas. After that, she could put those ideas into an outline. The next step would be writing a very rough draft; then she would write a better draft; then she would proofread for spelling, punctuation, etc.; and finally she would write the version to be handed in. It is a good idea not to do too many steps at one time—they should be spread over a few days. Also, it is really hard to proofread something immediately after writing it; it's best to proofread one or two nights after writing the last version.

to remember many different things at the same time, organize your ideas, and get others to understand them. Having these abilities will be helpful in any job.

MATHEMATICS

Mathematics is another subject that teaches you a lot about remembering and thinking and organizing your ideas. We'll now explore mathematics to find out what it takes to do it well and what kinds of weaknesses make mathematics hard for certain students.

Those Who Love Math and Those Who Don't

Some lucky kids have a special feel for mathematics. The whole subject just makes sense to them. They find it easy to learn new math ideas and to be accurate when solving all different kinds of math problems. Not only can they do well on tests in mathematics, but they are able to use what they learn in everyday life—when they do things like buy something at a store, figure out how long a car trip will take, or estimate how much money they'll have in the bank by the end of the year.

Unfortunately, not everyone loves math. There are some students who find it rough. Too many of the facts and concepts are either too hard to understand or too hard to remember or too hard to use (or all three things). These students can fall very far behind in their mathematics skills. Many of them then start to hate math. They find math classes embarrassing. In fact, it is not unusual for a student to become *afraid* of mathematics.

PIZZA SPECIAL
1 slice $1.25
2 slices $2.40
3 slices $3.65
½ pie $4.25

A student who is really good at mathematics is able to apply what he or she learns with great ease. This girl is trying to figure out how many slices of pizza she can afford. To do so, she is using her very best mathematical abilities (with some difficulty).

During math classes, he may feel as if he is locked inside a cage with a wild animal!

In many other subjects, there is more than one right answer to a problem or teacher's question. For instance, there are a lot of interesting ways to write a book report, and there are many ways to describe what's been read in a social studies chapter. On a math test, however, there is usually only one correct answer for each problem. Many students have brains that need more freedom. Their brains feel uncomfortable with problems for which there is only one right answer. Often that kind of student doesn't get along too well in mathematics classes.

Abilities Needed To Do Math

Mathematics, just like writing, forces us to use a mixture of many different functions and abilities that we have either acquired over the years or that we were born with. In mathematics classes, a student has to interpret complicated language, understand abstract concepts (verbally and non-verbally), sequence steps in the right order, visualize or picture things, pay close attention to detail, be a good problem solver and have a memory that works pretty quickly and accurately. Because of this, many different regions of the brain have to work well together if someone is to succeed in mathematics classes.

Problems That Students Have with Math

What kinds of troubles can cause a student to do poorly in math or to learn to fear and hate it? We will look at several possibilities.

- **Trouble Number One: Grasping the Concepts.** Mathematics is loaded with concepts. You may remember that we talked about concepts in Chapter 5. Let's review: a concept is a kind of idea that brings together into one group a number of other facts, ideas, or even other concepts. For example, the concept of furniture includes beds, desks, tables, and chairs. In mathematics, the concepts include things like number, place value, percentage, decimal, and equation. Once you understand these math concepts, it makes it easier to use them in a whole series of *operations*.

The word *operations* may make you think of something a surgeon does (such as removing your appendix). Actually, operations in mathematics can be compared to surgery. In math, you take some numbers, and you operate on them using facts and concepts as tools. If you don't understand the concepts, or if you barely understand the concepts, your scalpel won't be very sharp, so the operation may not be too successful. In medicine, common operations include removing an appendix or the tonsils. In mathematics, common operations are multiplication, division, subtraction, and other processes like them.

As you go from grade to grade, mathematics gets much harder. Each year you have to remember old concepts and add a lot of new ones. Students differ from one another in terms of how fast they can grasp (really understand and hold onto) the steady flow of new concepts. Some students catch on quickly and have an excellent understanding of new concepts. Others catch on too slowly and even then the concepts may feel slippery—they may be too hard to grasp.

The following list consists of various statements that a student could make about a concept. Each one shows you the ways a person may or may not grasp the concept. The farther down the list you go, the stronger the person's grasp of the concept. A strong grasp means that a student knows the concept well and can use it in math work.

1. "I don't get it."

2. "I can remember and repeat the math concept just the way the teacher said it."

3. "I can explain the math concept in my own words or picture it clearly in my mind."

4. "I could teach someone else the math concept."

5. "I can use the math concept to solve problems in school or on homework."

6. "I am now using this math concept in my everyday life— even outside school."

7. "I can think of some new uses for this math concept— uses no one ever taught me."

Think about different concepts in mathematics and try to decide how strong your grasps are. Also, when you learn a new concept, think about your grasp on that new concept. If it is a pretty loose grasp, you need to think of ways of making it stronger.

- **Trouble Number Two: A Weak Mathematics Memory.** Mathematics requires a lot of memory. You have to remember your addition and subtraction facts such as $4 - 2$ or $8 + 7$. Multiplication tables can be a big strain on your memory when you're first learning them. They may be the biggest memory strain that you've ever had. Not only do you have to remember addition, subtraction, and multiplication facts, but you have to be able to remember them very quickly. When you're solving a complicated mathematics problem, you can't take too long to recall how much 8×7 is. The number 56 has to pop up from your automatic memory without taking up much of your time, attention, or brain energy. Once again, you need your old friend automatized memory (discussed in Chapter 3). If you take too long to recall 8×7, you might forget something else you need to do.

Mathematics also requires *active working memory* (also discussed in Chapter 3). When you finish doing one part of a math problem, you need to remember what it was that you were going to do next. For example, while you are solving a word problem, you may multiply two numbers. While doing the multiplication, you shouldn't forget why you are multiplying the numbers or how you are going to use the answer to the multiplication to solve the whole problem. In fact, very often when you solve a problem, you have to do one part of the problem, then the next part, and then return to the first part of the problem. In other words, you have to hold a lot of information on that "wide screen" inside your mind while you are working on it. (We compared memory to a screen in Chapters 2 and 3.) You can't lose track of what you are doing. Unfortunately, the memory screens of some students are too small, or things fade from them too quickly.

Students who have trouble with memory in mathematics can be helped in a lot of different ways. Some kids need to use a calculator while they solve problems. Doing this gives them some extra memory. Other students need to write down as much as they can and do as little mathematics in their heads as possible. Still others need to do a lot of drill and practice so that they can remember their basic math facts more quickly and accurately. This could be compared to oiling or greasing a motor.

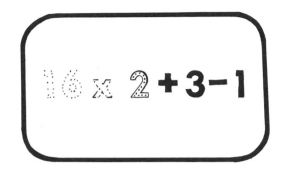

Some students have trouble remembering all the parts of a problem while they are working on it. In this case, a teacher has asked: "How much is $16 \times 2 + 3 - 1$?" You can see how the first numbers are starting to fade from the student's memory by the time the teacher gets to the last numbers. When this happens often, a student may be said to have weak active working memory, *and that student can get into serious difficulty in mathematics.*

- **Trouble Number Three: Poor Understanding of the Language of Mathematics.** There is a lot of language in a math class. The teacher explains things in words and sentences. Fortunately, he or she also writes examples on the chalkboard. This means you can compare what is being said with what you see. This helps, especially if you are the kind of student who prefers to learn through your eyes. Still, there are some kids who get confused about language in mathematics classes. They have difficulty keeping up with what the teacher is saying. They may also have trouble understanding certain assignments. Language in mathematics (and in science) is densely packed. That means a whole lot of important ideas get said in a short time or in a small space on a page.

  But in mathematics classes, probably more than in any other class, important facts, concepts, and operations get explained more than once. So a student has to realize that if he doesn't get something the first time, or even the second or third time, he should just stay tuned in because the concept will come up again! Maybe what he needs to do is tune in with stronger attention. Unfortunately, some kids behave in just the opposite way. If they don't understand something, they tune out and give up. This means that they'll never get the concept the next time it comes around!

Some students with weak language skills get into difficulty especially with word problems. They have trouble understanding just what's being asked. It's hard for them to tell what's important and what's not. They may have trouble translating the words of a problem into specific mathematics operations such as addition, multiplication, or division. These students often prefer worksheets where they make calculations directly without having to figure them out from word problems.

In fact, it is possible to be very good at math but not too good with language. Many students with language disorders try to change concepts into pictures. Instead of reading about them or trying to understand an explanation by the teacher, some kids prefer looking at a correctly solved problem. In mathematics, as in many subjects, you can use your strengths to overcome your weaknesses.

- **Trouble Number Four: Poor Problem-Solving Skills.** Problem solving is an important part of mathematics. It has to do with thinking up the best way (or ways) to come up with a correct answer. Word problems, calculations, and everyday situations where you need to use your mathematics all demand good problem-solving abilities. When you're up against a hard math problem, you are like a detective; you have to find clues and you have to think of different possible solutions until you find the right one. That means you have to take your time and do a lot of planning and careful thinking. There are some crucial steps involved in being a good problem solver. These were mentioned in Chapter 5. For now, let us pretend for a moment that we are solving a problem on a math test.

The following questions make up a series of steps that a good problem solver would go through to get the right answer.

1. What is being asked for in this problem?

2. What hints or clues am I given about how to solve this problem? Do certain words or symbols make me think of certain operations like addition or multiplication?

3. What facts or concepts will I have to look up in my memory to solve this problem?

4. What is a rough estimate of the answer to this problem?

5. Of all the methods I can think of to solve this problem, what is the best one to try first?

6. Now that I have tried that method, does it feel right; did it work?

7. If my method did not work, what other method should I try next?

8. Am I finished? If I am, does the answer look right?

If you think about good problem solving, you will see that a good problem solver "hangs loose." She or he doesn't jump to conclusions, but instead goes slowly. He or she is willing to come up with tentative solutions. The word *tentative* means "temporary"; it means that a change of mind is possible. Often when a student is a poor problem solver, that student moves too quickly, makes up his mind too fast, and doesn't think up other possibilities just in case his way of doing things turns out to be the wrong way. It may seem odd, but often an expert problem solver takes much longer to solve problems than a beginner or poor problem solver. It is possible to improve as a problem solver. Many students have to work on being better at planning and thinking about problems before they rush ahead and solve them.

- **Trouble Number Five: Visualizing.** In mathematics, there are a lot of concepts that are hard to put into words. Many of these concepts can be learned better if you can picture them or think about them without having to use too much language. Concepts such as proportion or fraction are important to picture. (See the illustration on page 191.) Some mathematical learning involves understanding shapes, sizes, and dimensions. Concepts such as parallelogram, trapezoid, perimeter, and diameter can be tricky to understand unless you can see clear pictures or images of them in your brain. Some students form excellent images or pictures while others have to put everything into words. If all you can do is describe a shape in words, if you can never make a good picture of it, you probably will not have a very strong grasp of that shape and all its characteristics. A really good mathematician can go back and forth from words to pictures, using one to strengthen the other. So, if you are weak in visualizing, you should practice trying to "see" what you are able to describe in words.

Fraction $= \frac{1}{4}$

Proportion

Some math students are excellent at picturing important concepts in that subject. When a teacher mentions something, a student imagines a visual image of the idea. The boy in this illustration is able to visualize fractions and proportions. This ability helps him understand and remember the concepts.

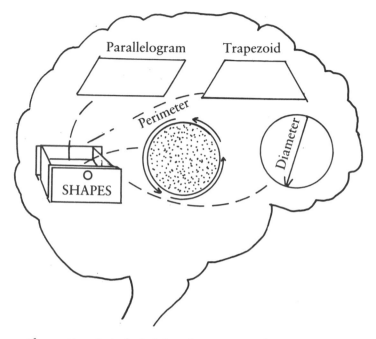

For mathematics, it is helpful to have a good visual memory. You need to be able to visualize and remember how different shapes actually look. When somebody says the word trapezoid, *you need to be able to picture that particular shape by finding it in your memory.*

- **Trouble Number Six: Remembering Things in the Right Order.** Mathematics tests your sequencing ability. This is your ability to put things, do things, or keep things in the correct order. For example, to count from one to ten, you must present the numbers in a definite order, or what you say will not be correct. Teachers often explain mathematical operations in a particular order. When solving math problems, you usually have to do the right steps in the right order or your answer will not be right.

Many students with sequencing problems have trouble learning the multiplication tables. It might take them an extra year or two to store those tables in their memories and even longer to learn them well enough for answers to come automatically during problem solving. In Chapter 5, we saw that some students with sequencing problems get mixed up about time. They are late learning how to tell time, and late learning the days of the week and the months of the year. These students also can have trouble with time concepts in math class. Word problems that have time in them might be especially confusing for them.

Like other kids with problems, those with sequencing problems—if they know they have such problems—can work on them. They need to work hard on doing and arranging things in the right order, taking good notes, making lists, and working with calendars, clocks, and other devices to get themselves organized in terms of time.

- **Trouble Number Seven: Attention to Detail.** Mathematics is full of little details. In order to be accurate in solving math problems, you have to be very alert and tuned in. Therefore, things like attentional problems (which we discussed in Chapter 2) may cause trouble for you. You may find that you keep missing little but important details, such as the difference between a plus sign and a minus sign. If you have a problem like this, you will make a lot of careless mistakes, even though you may have a good grasp of mathematics concepts and an excellent mathematics memory.

As we have seen, many students with attention problems work impulsively or too quickly. If they work this way in math, they will make loads of silly mistakes. They won't be good problem solvers because they won't spend enough time planning and thinking of different methods to use to solve a problem. Also, many kids with attention deficits are poor at self-monitoring. They don't go back over their work to make sure that it's correct. It's hard for them to estimate an answer and then compare it to the one they finally get. This is another reason that they make careless mistakes.

Students with attention deficits need to work on their attention deficits. Mathematics is a very good subject for doing this because it involves so much detail and requires so much planning and thinking in advance of doing. If a student wants to cut down on impulsiveness, he or she should try to solve a math problem slowly as a way of building planning strength in the brain. Or, a student could be helped by having a tutor or teacher say: "Here's a problem you usually do in twenty seconds. I want to see if you know how to do this problem in two minutes." Or, the student could work on his or her attention by going through the individual steps of problem solving for a particular problem and writing them out or recording them on tape. There are also exercises that kids can use to help themselves with proofreading, or self-monitoring, and attention to detail. For example, it can be helpful to correct other people's papers or to get an adult to provide the student with a page of math problems (some with mistakes) to check over. All of these activities can help students who are struggling with their attention.

- **Trouble Number Eight: Not Recognizing or Not Admitting a Lack of Understanding.** Some kids have trouble knowing whether they really understand something in mathematics. Others have a hard time admitting their lack of understanding to themselves or others, so they pretend to understand more

Some students feel as if they are on "top of" mathematics, while others have a sense that they are buried under heaps of confusing numbers. For them, mathematics is a huge burden. They think they'll never catch up. Sometimes students become so afraid of mathematics that they just give up.

than they really do. Such students get further and further behind in math.

Mathematics concepts, operations, and facts pile up. In some courses such as English and social studies, new topics come up, and in order to understand them you do not always have to remember what went before them. This is not true in mathematics, however. In math, you must understand and remember basic concepts in order to understand the new ones that you will keep meeting in school. This means that you must stay alert. When you feel yourself getting behind, you have to be honest with yourself and your teacher before you start feeling buried under a heap of mixed up numbers.

Not everybody can be a great mathematician. Those whose brains seem to specialize in mathematics learn a lot and have fun with numbers. But others can be fairly good too. The most important thing is not to be afraid of math and not to let yourself get too far behind.

OTHER SUBJECTS

In this book, we really do not have the time or the space to write about every school subject. However, by now, you probably realize that all subjects involve different combinations of the skills and functions that we have already discussed. Social studies, science, music, art, foreign language, and health are all, in a way, like recipes in a cookbook. Each contains its own ingredients, and each requires you to carry out specific procedures. As you study different subjects, try to think about them in terms of the different functions and skills that you must use. If you end up having problems in a subject, try to figure out which of your functions is weak. Your parents, teachers, or other adults can help you do this. Once you know your problem, you can come up with some ways of working around it. One of the most exciting triumphs for a student is bouncing back from failure or near failure. Instead of getting discouraged, try to understand the reasons you have fallen behind and the ways you might make up for lost time.

CHAPTER SEVEN

The Social Side of School

DOUG'S STORY

Doug is used to being unpopular—he has never been liked by other kids. In fact, all through school, other students have called him names, bullied him, and stayed away from him. For a while he was known as "Doug the bug." At the bus stop, a favorite game was called "Let's bug Doug the bug." Sometimes when he was teased, Doug would get real angry and start fighting and cursing. Some of the other kids thought that was funny and actually enjoyed trying to set him off.

Doug often comes home from school feeling upset. He once liked school, but he doesn't anymore. Even though he gets good grades, the school day is extremely tense for him. No one wants to sit next to him on the school bus or at lunch. The kids say he's a "geek," "nerd," and "wimp." He hates these words and tries to ignore other kids when they use them to describe him, but the name calling still hurts him a lot inside.

Doug is interested in many things. He likes science fiction, video games, and computers. He's interested in collecting rocks and comic books. In fact, he loves buying comic books. He has read his over and over again and has become a real expert on all kinds of comic book characters. Other kids think Doug's interests are weird. Many of them talk about clothes and music. Doug is not at all interested in what kind of clothes he wears, in how he looks, in buying cassettes at the mall, or in sports. Doug's sister, who is very popular, wants Doug to act more "cool" and less like a "dork." Doug really doesn't understand what she means by "cool."

To add to his problems, Doug keeps saying the wrong things. Or, he says things at the wrong times. When other kids are trying to be serious, Doug will crack a joke. When other kids are having fun, Doug will say something serious or sad. When Doug starts talking about something that interests him, he doesn't know when to stop. Everyone else gets bored when he talks on and on, but Doug doesn't notice. Also, when Doug says or does something that makes others think that he's strange, he doesn't realize it. He just doesn't pick up "signals" from other kids, the kinds of signals that mean he needs to change what he's saying or doing to avoid annoying the other kids. Because he doesn't get the signals, Doug's reputation keeps getting worse and worse.

Doug has no idea why nobody likes him. He'd like to have friends, and he'd like to be more popular, but he doesn't know how to do it. Also, he sort of likes himself the way he is. He would rather not have to change all of his interests and his whole personality just to get some friends. He once asked his sister: "Why does everyone in school have to be the same to be accepted?" Doug's guidance counselor has told him that he lacks social skills. Such a problem means that Doug doesn't know some things that other kids do—what a kid has to say or do to make and keep friends and to have a decent reputation.

Doug's parents think that their son is a very interesting boy who could become a very successful adult. They are actually pleased that their son doesn't try to be like everybody else. But Doug's parents realize how unhappy Doug is. They realize that he would like to have friends and not be alone all the time. They are wondering how a boy like Doug can keep being different from other kids and still have friends and be pretty popular. Doug also wonders about this.

Thinking More about Doug

Try answering the following questions about Doug after reading all of Chapter 7.

- Which social skills that make kids popular are a problem for Doug?
- Should Doug try to be more like other kids, or should he just be himself? Is it possible to have "weird" interests and still be well-liked by other kids?

MAKING FRIENDS AND BEING POPULAR

When you first think about it, school seems to be just a place where you go to learn facts, concepts, and skills from books and teachers. But there is another side of school that is just as important. This side doesn't get talked about nearly as much as the academic side. It is the social side of school, the side that has to do with making friends, being popular, and learning how to be part of the world of your own age group. This social side can be one of the hardest but also one of the most exciting parts of school.

What Kids Think of Each Other

One problem every kid has in school is lack of privacy. All day long you are watched, tested, and judged by other kids. They are trying to make up their minds about you. They are deciding what kind of person they think you are and whether they want to get to know you better. They are deciding whether they like you or admire you. When other students like you and enjoy being with you, you feel good, and life at school is fun. Some students find it very easy to be socially successful. Other kids find social skills one of the hardest subjects in school.

Two Kinds of Social Success

There are two kinds of social success: 1) having friends, and 2) being popular. It is possible to have close friends without being popular. Believe it or not, it is also possible to be popular without having any close friends. Having close friends means that there are kids that you get to know very well. It means that you can keep up a relationship over a long time and that you can share feelings, activities, and trust. Being popular means having a good reputation. It means that many other kids respect you and like you, even if they don't know you very well. It might mean that you get elected to a class office, or that you get invited to a lot of parties, or that your telephone rings all the time at home.

Degrees of Popularity

The opposite of having friends is being a "loner." The opposite of popularity is rejection. Between popularity and rejection, there are some other possibilities. For example, a student may be controversial—popular with some groups of kids but not with others. Or, there are some students who are very quiet and don't know very many people. They are "neglected" by the other kids; they are not popular, but they are not rejected either—they are in between.

Popularity Tests

Just as there are tests in math, English, and social studies, there are tests in the social side of school. These tests take place at the bus stop, on the school bus, in the corridors, in the cafeteria, and on the playground. These places are the big social hotspots. Here you find out whether other students accept you, neglect you, or reject you—whether they want to stand or sit next to you. It is here that some kids get picked on, made fun of, or ignored. Here, it is easy either to feel proud or badly embarrassed. Failing a social test can be much more painful than failing a spelling test! Kids who keep failing socially can become sad and frightened in school, even if they are doing well in their regular subjects.

SKILLS NEEDED FOR SOCIAL SUCCESS

In earlier chapters in this book, we discussed the functions (like attention, language, and memory) that you need to do well in reading, writing, spelling, and mathematics. Social success also requires certain skills. On the following pages we will explore four kinds of skills needed for social success at school and in your neighborhood. The four skills are 1) Starting up Relationships, 2) Keeping up Relationships, 3) Getting and Using the Right Social Feedback, 4) Speaking and Understanding Social Language.

Starting Up Relationships

Knowing How To Fit In: Developing a new relationship can be tough, but with skill it can be done smoothly. Let's suppose that there are two kids talking in the corridor. One of them says to the other: "I sure wish we didn't have to write that book report tonight. I hate book reports. They're really dumb." The other one says: "Yeah, I haven't even read the book yet. I don't know when I'm gonna do the book report. She gives us too much to write. It's just not fair."

If you want to enter a relationship with those two kids who were just talking, what should you do? First of all, you should listen to what they are saying and notice their feelings and their points of view. If you want to get them to accept you, if you want to fit in with them, you should say something that would match their feelings. You might say: "She gives us too many tests too. The other English class has no book reports and almost no tests." That would be excellent. It would show that you can understand and share feelings with the other two students.

Some kids have trouble reading the feelings and attitudes of other kids. A student who has that kind of social skills problem might say: "I think book reports are very good for us. I learn something every time I write one. Tests are also good because they make us study hard and teach us to use our memories well." This student may be perfectly correct in everything she or he has said, but this student is in trouble socially! He or she did not know how to "read" feelings and start a relationship going smoothly by agreeing with the others.

Not Being Too Direct: Another part of starting up relationships requires you not to say and do things that are too obvious or direct. If there is a student in your class whom you want to become friends with, how should you do it? A good way might be to walk up to that student and say: "How would you like to go to the mall this weekend? A few of us are going to have lunch at the mall. Would you like to go with us?" By saying that, you have really told that student that you like him or her and that you want to form a friendship.

A student with poor social skills might walk up to the kid and say: "I like you. I'm a nice kid and so are you. How about us being friends from now on? I think we could be great together. Let's be friends from now on." This very direct and honest approach doesn't work. You have to be slower and less obvious.

Not Rushing Things: It is especially important not to rush things. When you first meet someone, you can't act the same way you would act with someone you've known for years. You can't just meet someone and a few minutes later try to borrow money, tease, boast and do other things that you might try only on someone you know really well. Kids with poor social skills may try to be very friendly with everyone, but they don't make real friends very easily. Sometimes this is because they rush their relationships.

Choosing the Group That's Right for You: Another important part of starting up a relationship is figuring out common interests. If you want to be part of a group, for example, you have to understand the interests of its members. You also have to think about the kinds of things you like to do. Then you must decide whether or not you would fit in. It's great to be accepted by other kids, but it can also be a problem if you have to do or say things you don't like just to be accepted. Doing that has led many students into serious problems. You need to look for kids whose interests are not too far from your own so you can share in activities that you enjoy. Some students with social skills problems have trouble figuring out what other people are interested in, so they may not be able to fit themselves into the right group or in with the right friend.

Keeping Up Relationships

Once relationships start up, they need to be kept up. Having friends is like having a garden. Not only do you have to plant seeds in the soil of a garden, but also you have to keep watering the plants to keep them alive. Once you begin a friendship, you have to keep working at it to make it last.

Thinking of the Other Person: To keep up friendships, you have to think about what friends need or want from you. You should be able to put yourself into a friend's place and imagine how you would feel if you were that person. Then you need to say things that make a friend feel good. If you find yourself boasting or bragging, you need to praise the person or people you are with, just to keep things in balance. If all you think and talk about is yourself, a relationship can fall apart.

Dealing with Disagreements: An important part of holding on to friendships is knowing what to do when a friendship is in trouble. Whenever two or more people get together, sooner or later there is bound to be a disagreement or an argument. When this happens, the important questions are: How can the disagreement be handled? If an argument has occurred and caused damage to the friendship, how can the damage be repaired? A socially skilled kid has good ideas for dealing with such problems. If a disagreement exists, he or she might compromise or figure out something to do that will take everyone's mind off the problem for a while. If an argument has occurred, a socially skilled person might suggest talking things out. This way everyone involved could express his or her feelings.

Unfortunately, a lot of kids with poor social skills have trouble figuring out what to do when things are going badly in a relationship. They are more likely to shout, criticize, use bad words, get revenge, or fight. Such behavior only makes things worse. It puts them in danger of losing a friend forever.

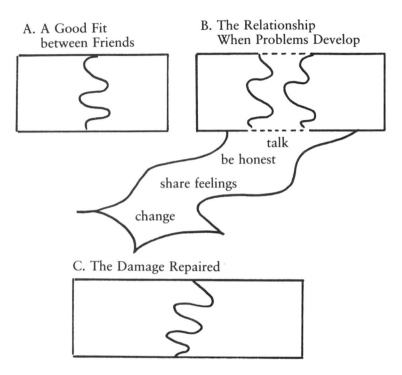

A. A Good Fit between Friends

B. The Relationship When Problems Develop

talk
be honest
share feelings
change

C. The Damage Repaired

It is impossible for friends to get along well all of the time. Relationships come apart sometimes. In the diagram above, you can see that what looks like a nice fit between two friends may come apart. In order to repair the damage in the relationship, the friends have to talk, be honest with each other, exchange their true feelings, and try to make changes so they can repair their damaged friendship.

Getting and Using the Right Social Feedback

In order to keep up relationships, you have to know how you're doing. You need to get feedback from other people, so you can steer relationships in the right direction. Let's now look at how feedback works.

Picking Up Social Feedback Cues: Whenever we are with other people, we need to keep our "antennas" raised, so that we can pick up signals that tell us how we are doing in the relationship. These signals are called social feedback cues. You might pick up these signals by watching the expression on someone's face. You can sometimes tell how someone feels about you by watching for little things that are said (or not said). There are many unpopular students who don't pick up social feedback cues. They say and do things that other people just don't like, but they miss the feedback, the looks on people's faces, the comments they make.

Some students with attentional disorders (which we talked about in Chapter 2) have trouble with all kinds of feedback. They are not good at self-monitoring when they do their schoolwork, and they are not good at self-monitoring in their relationships either. On the other hand, some kids are great at watching and listening for the reactions of other people. They keep getting a second chance when something goes wrong.

Recovering from Your Mistakes: Once you receive feedback, you can do something about it if you need to. You can recover from your mistakes. But, you need to know how to do this. Socially skilled kids have this knowledge. If they've said something to make someone else angry, they might apologize. If they say something that at first sounds weird, they might add something to what they have said so that it will sound better.

Let's look at an example of using social feedback in school. Pretend that on Monday a teacher tells the class that it is going to have a test on Thursday. One kid raises his hand and says: "Why can't we have the test on Tuesday instead?" He is saying that to impress the teacher with how ready he is for the test.

Puzzled   Happy

Speechless   Angry

Social Feedback Cues: An important part of social skills is the ability to know how you're doing when you are with someone else. You need to be "tuned in" to social feedback cues. A person who has social abilities is constantly watching and listening to other people's reactions to what she or he is doing or saying. That way, if someone is unhappy with the socially skilled person, he or she knows it right away and can make a change in behavior to maintain a good relationship. Some kids with social feedback problems keep missing the social feedback cues, and so their relationships suffer.

Now, if he looks around at the other students in the class, he will probably see that many of them are annoyed and angry at him for suggesting that the test be two days earlier. If he is able to pick up social feedback cues, he will realize that he has just said something that could get him into big social trouble with the other students. He can then say: "Aw, I was just kidding." Or, he might say: "I meant the Tuesday *after* Thursday; I meant next Tuesday, not tomorrow." Absolutely everybody makes social mistakes. The important questions are: Do you know when you've made one, and then do you know what to do about it?

Understanding Your Social Image: Another part of getting and using feedback has to do with understanding how your behavior and your appearance are viewed by other people. How you dress, what you do, and what you are interested in are all part of your special "image." In order to succeed socially, you need to understand your image or how you look or seem to other kids. Some students with social problems have no idea of how they appear to other kids.

In terms of image, there are two dangers. One is being so "out of it" that you have no idea of how you affect others. The other is being so "tuned in" to getting other kids to like the way you look and act that you are afraid just to be yourself. You lose all your specialness that way. We'll talk more about this problem later. What you want to aim for is a balanced position.

Another part of image development has to do with the things you say and the ways you say them. Therefore, language becomes an important part of social life. Let's now consider how social language works.

Speaking and Understanding Social Language

The way you talk tells people a lot about the kind of person you are. Other kids listen to you and try to figure you out as they hear your ideas and the words and sentences you use to say them.

Knowing the "Right" Words: Popular students are often very good with the "in" language that they hear other kids using in school. They are up to date when it comes to meanings of terms like *awesome, rad, cool, nerd,* or *dork.* New terms come up from year to year, and they can vary from town to town. This special language usually is one that grown-ups don't use or understand too well. A kid, however, is supposed to keep up with the latest fads in such lingo and use "cool" words easily and at the right times. Doing this proves that he or she is part of the social scene and not just part of a family at home. Some kids with social problems have trouble using the "right" words in the right way. When they talk, they don't sound very "cool." Often because they don't receive good social feedback cues, they don't even realize that the way they talk is creating problems for them.

Communicating Your Feelings: Another part of social language has to do with using words and sentences to let people know how you feel. Feelings can be hard to communicate, and when it comes to feelings, students with social language problems are sometimes misunderstood. For example, people may think that they're angry when they are not, because the way they say things makes them sound angry. Or, the way a kid talks may make other kids think he doesn't like them—when he really *does* like them. Such a kid has problems putting true feelings into language. He or she also might have trouble understanding the true feelings of others when *they* talk. He or she might mistake pleasure for annoyance. This, too, can cause serious misunderstandings.

Making Language Fit the Situation: Another part of social language is called *code switching*. It has to do with your ability to change the way you talk depending upon where you are and to whom you're talking. You wouldn't talk the same way with your best friend, your grandmother, your little sister (if you have one), or a police officer. You need to know how to switch from one code to another. Since many students with social language problems have trouble doing this, they often say things that don't sound right.

Choosing a Topic: Another important part of social language is talking about the right thing at the right time. This is called *topic selection*. What you talk about should depend upon the social scene you're in. Topic selection can be a real challenge. It can sometimes be hard to figure out what to discuss with a kid you've just met. Likewise, it's difficult to select a topic when you are with some students whom you don't know very well but whom you would like to get to know better. Some kids with social problems talk about the wrong things. Or, they talk about things at the wrong times. They pick topics that seem "weird" or not connected to what's going on at the moment.

Knowing When To Stop Talking: An ability related to topic selection is *topic maintenance*. It has to do with how long you talk about something. Some kids with social language problems don't know when to stop. They talk about something for so long that it gets boring. Of course, if someone like that were able to pick up social feedback cues, she or he would know when it is time to change topics.

KEEPING A SOCIAL LIFE IN BALANCE

Being *Too* Popular

As we have said, it is great fun to be popular, and it can be very painful to be rejected by other kids. But, is it possible to be too popular? Is it possible to need friends too much? The answer is yes. There are some students who are so hungry for the approval and respect of other kids that they will do almost anything to make and keep friends or to gain an excellent reputation. There are some very popular students who end up doing poorly in school because all they care about is their friends. They are so distracted by other students that they can't concentrate on school work.

Keeping Social Life in Balance: *It is very important to keep a social life in balance. Kids who are too popular, too busy with each other, may start doing poorly in school. On the other hand, students who have no friends are very sad and lonely much of the time. It is best to keep your social life well balanced—not to be too involved in it, but not to be a loner either.*

Conforming Too Much

Some kids feel that the only way to be popular is to be exactly like everyone else. They dress the same, they talk the same, they act the same, they pick up the same interests, and they do the same things on weekends. They are afraid to be different. These students are called conformists. They will do everything they can to avoid looking or acting "weird."

Sometimes students who are too concerned about being popular and "normal" do not develop their own special qualities. Then they can have an even bigger problem than students who are rejected. The students who are trying too hard to be popular may not really develop the right strengths and abilities to succeed in the adult world. Also, such students may find themselves doing things just to please other kids. That sometimes leads to some very serious problems like smoking, taking drugs, or even committing crimes. Often these kinds of acts are done mostly to impress other kids, to show them how grown-up, how "macho," how "cool," or how brave someone is. Problems like the ones just mentioned are pretty high prices to pay for popularity. They can cause you trouble that can last for many, many years.

Appreciating Your Individuality

Not everybody wants to be popular. Not everybody needs to be popular. Not everybody can be popular. There are some students who cherish their specialness, their individuality. They want to be themselves. They like being different. In some ways, they are heroes or heroines because it takes a certain amount of bravery to be yourself. At times, it can be lonely, but it may be worth it. It is okay to be socially independent as long as you really want to be. In fact, if someone is a loner by choice, he or she should probably be congratulated! Being a loner becomes a problem only if a kid is afraid of relationships or because she or he can't succeed socially.

Keeping a Balance

Often, the best social life is the one that is neither the life of a loner nor the life of an extremely popular person. As we said earlier, social life can be kept in balance. A student can be popular and still be a unique person. He or she can have friends without imitating everyone else all the time. There are students who have the courage to have unusual interests, to wear clothes they like even if they're not what everyone else likes, and to express their ideas even if other kids might not agree with them. A socially skilled person is able to keep a balance between trying too hard to be popular and being a loner. This balance is worth trying to achieve because it can make you happy during school while it strengthens your social skills.

Social Life Checklist

Starting Up Relationships
- "Read" other kids—understand how they feel about things.
- Show others that you share their feelings.
- Go slowly enough—try not to rush a relationship.
- Find common interests and come up with good things to do together.

Keeping Up Relationships
- Make the other person feel good—be able to praise someone else. Don't boast or brag too much.
- Know a lot of ways to fix a damaged relationship.

Getting and Using the Right Social Feedback
- Get social feedback cues—know how someone else is feeling about what you are doing or saying.
- Understand your own image and how it is working with other people.
- Know how to change your image—if you really want to change it.

Speaking and Understanding Social Language
- Know how to speak the language of kids your age.
- Communicate your true feelings when you speak.
- Figure out other people's true feelings when they speak.
- Use the right language code at the right time, in the right place, with the right people.
- Pick the best topics to talk about and know when it's a good time to change the subject.
- Be able to use language to persuade or influence others and to settle arguments or differences.

Keeping a Social Life in Balance
- Be your true self. Don't be a complete conformist or a phony just so that other kids will like you.
- Achieve a balanced reputation—be popular but not too popular. Be a true individual but not a loner (unless you want to be).
- Don't let a social life become so important that nothing else seems to matter very much. This will hurt you in the long run.
- Try for an excellent reputation without rejecting or picking on kids with social skills problems.

DEALING WITH SOCIAL PROBLEMS

What can be done for a student who has trouble with his or her social skills, a student who would like to be more popular and have more or closer friends? The life of a rejected student is often very sad. Bullies may say and do things that hurt and embarrass a rejected kid. If you fall into this category, every day can be painful, as other students call you names, push you around, refuse to include you, or whisper about you. It can be especially difficult when you have a brother or sister who's popular, when the phone rings all the time for him or her and almost never for you, when there are lots of invitations to parties for other members of your family but none for you. This is a sad situation and a common one. Fortunately, there are things that can be done about it.

Understanding Social Rejection

First of all, you need to understand *why* social rejection is happening. Are there certain social skills that you just don't seem to have? As you read through this chapter, did you find certain things that are real problems for you? Second, if kids are making fun of you, how are they doing it? Do they make fun of your name? Is it the way you look? Do they think of you as too fat, too skinny, too weird looking, or too clumsy at sports? Are there certain bullies in school who keep giving you a hard time? Is it possible that some students are jealous of you, of something you have, of something you do, or of your skill? There are some kids who may deal with their envy by being mean. If you have learning disorders, are other kids making fun of you because of your problem? Do they tease you about getting extra help in school? What are the exact names or terms they use when they make fun of you? In other words, to begin getting help with your social problems, you have to start out by being a detective; you have to figure out exactly what is happening and why it's happening.

Getting Help

You should never have to face social problems all by yourself. It's scary to be tripped in front of your locker, have your books fall all over the floor and get kicked by another kid while a whole bunch of students laugh at you.

Instead of keeping such an experience inside yourself, you should talk about it to your parents or to some other adult. You need someone who will give you time alone with him or her to talk about what happened and help you figure out what to do about it. The adults you talk to should not preach to you; they should help you think about the problem. A guidance counselor, a psychologist, a physician, a clergyperson, or an adult relative may be able to assist you in figuring out where your social skills are not working.

In more and more towns, there are people who specialize in social skills training. Sometimes they take a group of kids who are having social problems and coach them on social skills, such as starting and keeping up relationships, getting and using the right feedback, speaking and understanding social language, and keeping a social life in balance. This kind of training can really help kids for whom social skills don't come naturally. With enough interest and work, anybody can improve his or her social abilities.

In school, a kid with social skills problems should stand up for his or her own rights. Sometimes you can do this by letting your teacher, assistant principal, or principal know that you have a problem. The school may need to help you deal with bullying and with name calling. Sometimes it's necessary for the principal or head of the school to have a talk with some kids about the ways in which they are rejecting and embarrassing other kids. Sometimes kids who are very successful in social skills need to understand the serious harm they can do to rejected kids. The popular kids should know, too, that they can be really heroic if they try to help out and protect a classmate who is having a lot of social problems!

BUILDING CLOSE FRIENDSHIPS

A student with social skills problems should concentrate on finding and building one or two close friendships. In the long run, having these is more important than being popular with everyone. In trying to make friends it is important to search for kids that have some of the same interests that you do. Sharing activities is an important way to start a relationship and keep it going. Sometimes it is good to start with a friend who is a little younger or a bit older than you. The hardest thing is to form relationships with people your own age. Eventually, though, you do need to succeed with others your own age.

THE POSITIVE SIDE OF SOCIAL PROBLEMS

Finally, it is really important that unpopular students realize that because they are unpopular, they may be spending more time than other kids figuring out how to deal with problems. In other words, they may be getting a better preparation for being adults. It often turns out that when a popular child grows up, he or she ends up working for someone who was quite unpopular during childhood. If you are unpopular and you are looking around at popular kids, consider the possibility that they may want you to hire them sometime in the future!

CHAPTER EIGHT

Some Good Questions
(And Some Pretty Good Answers)

MELISSA AND DEBBIE: THEIR STORIES

Melissa is a worrier. She worries too much. She worries about school, about her health, and about whether other kids really like her. Melissa's parents say that she's too moody. They wish she wouldn't be so sad. They wish she would have more confidence in herself. Before a test, Melissa is sure she's going to fail it no matter how much she studies. The truth is that she never fails a test; she does well in school. She doesn't seem to have any important learning disorders that interfere with her schoolwork. Even though she gets good grades, she still feels that other kids are smarter, more popular, and more attractive than she is. She just doesn't have much respect for herself.

Melissa has a very close friend named Debbie. Debbie has some significant learning disorders. She has difficulty with memory and language. She has had to struggle all the way through school. She has failed some subjects and she was kept back in fourth grade. But Debbie feels good about herself. She doesn't worry too much. Like everyone, she becomes sad sometimes, but she always bounces back. Debbie knows she has some learning disorders and that she's getting help for them. Everyone who knows Debbie admires her self-esteem. Everyone who knows Melissa wonders why her self-esteem is so low. It seems funny that Debbie has trouble in school but feels good about herself, while Melissa gets good grades but feels bad about herself!

Recently Debbie has been concerned about Melissa. Melissa seems sadder than ever. She has lost interest in her hobbies and feels tired all the time. Melissa used to like to go to parties and spend hours at the shopping mall on weekends. Now she keeps saying, "I don't feel like going. I think I'll stay home today." Melissa's parents are worried about her too. They think she might be depressed. They are planning to visit a psychologist who will help them understand Melissa better. Melissa will be able to get some advice from that psychologist about getting over her sadness.

Debbie likes Melissa a lot. She hopes Melissa will get over her depression so they can have fun again. From knowing Melissa, Debbie has learned something important. She has discovered that just about everyone has problems of some sort or other. She has realized that even kids who do well in school, even kids who have no learning disorders, can still have problems. She used to think that a student who is good looking, good at sports, popular, and smart must be free of problems. Melissa has taught her that you don't have to have a learning disorder to feel sad.

Thinking More about Melissa and Debbie

Try answering the following questions after reading Chapter 8.

- What would lead you to believe that Melissa is depressed?
- How can Debbie help Melissa improve her self-esteem?
- How can Melissa help Debbie with her language and memory problems?
- What is needed for any student to develop good self-esteem?

QUESTIONS AND ANSWERS

Kids with learning disorders usually have a lot of questions. Although these kids want—or need—answers to their questions, often they are too afraid or too embarrassed to ask the questions. Sometimes the problem is that the students can't decide how to word their questions or whom to ask about them. This chapter is written to help students by presenting the questions that many of them have on their minds. As you read this part of the book, you may recognize some facts and ideas that have been discussed earlier. This review should be helpful. What it will do is separate and highlight particular points to help students better understand themselves and others, and stress some things that students can do to be successful in school.

What Is a Learning Disability?

The term "learning disability" is often used by teachers and parents. *To say that someone has a learning disability means that the person has one or more weak brain functions that cause him or her to do poorly in school.* Schools often decide that a student has a learning *disability* if that student shows a big difference between a score on an intelligence test and a score on achievement tests (such as tests of reading, spelling, and arithmetic). But you can have learning *disorders* that do not show up on such tests. For example, a kid with attention deficits, motor problems, or social skills weaknesses may do well on tests of reading or mathematics, so the school may feel that she or he doesn't show a learning *disability* on tests, but that student still has one or more learning *disorders*. For this reason, we have not used the words "learning disability" very much in this book. Instead, we talk about "learning disorders."

Many scientists are studying learning disorders, trying to find out just what they are, where they originate in the brain, what causes them, and what can be done to help kids who have them. Every day there are new discoveries about learning disorders. Because we are finding out so much so fast, it's hard at this time to be sure about what we know! It is possible that a student may have a learning disorder that hasn't even been discovered yet. It is also true that just about everybody in the world has some kind of "learning disorder." No brain is perfect. It is just that some people have disorders that interfere with school. If your disorder makes it hard for you to whistle a tune, remember dance steps, or tie knots, it won't wreck your learning or school-work. But if your disorder makes it hard for you to decode words, you could end up with a serious reading problem (which causes much more trouble than a whistling problem).

What Is Attention Deficit Disorder (ADD)?

Many students are told that they have attention deficit disorder (sometimes shortened to ADD). *These kids are usually the ones who have difficulties with attention, the kinds of problems we described in Chapter 2. They have trouble concentrating; they are distractible; and they may do a lot of things too quickly and without careful thinking. Some of these kids are hyper-active, or overactive, but some are not.* Sometimes hyperactive kids are said to have ADHD (Attention Deficit Hyperactivity Disorder).

Not all students with attention deficits are the same. Most of them have one or more other kinds of learning disorders in addition to their attentional problems. Also, there are many reasons why someone may have trouble concentrating. Sometimes his attention is weak because he was born with weak attention. Sometimes her attention is weak because it doesn't do much good to concentrate if she can't understand what's going on or being said. Sometimes feelings or emotions get in the way when a person tries to concentrate.

What Is Dyslexia?

Dyslexia is another confusing word. A person who has "dyslexia" has learning disorders that make it hard for that person to read. *Dyslexia can affect a student's ability to decode individual words or to understand sentences and paragraphs.* There are many different kinds of reading problems, and some people call all of them *dyslexia*. Other people use the word *dyslexia* only to mean "trouble decoding single words." It is probably best just to call a reading problem a reading problem and then try to figure out which learning disorders are causing it and what can be done about it. This is less confusing than trying to know what different people mean by dyslexia.

What Does It Mean To Be Intelligent?

This is another tough question. *To be intelligent is to have the ability to understand, to learn, and to use what you learn and understand.* But, there are so many different ways to be intelligent or smart. Some kids are very intelligent at fixing and building things, while others are really smart with words. Some students are very intelligent in mathematics but seem to have real trouble with spelling or learning a foreign language. Good athletes are very intelligent in the ways they understand how to move their bodies through space and how to learn new gross motor skills. It is also possible to be very intelligent at music, art, or understanding other people and their personal problems.

When you grow up, it is possible to find a job and become very successful by using your own special kind of intelligence. Fortunately, most people become most interested in play or work that uses the kind of intelligence that is strongest for them. So, those who are very intelligent at figuring out how to play a sport usually like sports. People who are good at figuring out other people's personal problems like to help other people solve their personal problems. You don't have to be excellent in every area to be intelligent.

Are Students with Learning Disorders Sort of "Dumb"?

Many students with learning disorders believe they are not intelligent. There is a voice inside them that makes them think they are stupid or dumb. It is very easy to feel dumb when you find yourself in a classroom where everybody else appears to be learning easily, and you are having a hard time, or when you have to get special help that other kids don't seem to need. *Kids with learning disorders, however, are not dumb.*

As we have said, everybody has *some* weak brain function. It is also important to realize that everybody feels bad about himself or herself sometimes. We all get frustrated and wish we could be better at what we're trying to do. There is nothing abnormal about that. However, it is important to bounce back, to recover from feeling dumb and get your confidence again. If you don't bounce back, you may start to feel hopeless and stop trying to succeed. Then you'll never be able to overcome your weaknesses. Most kids grow up and overcome or bypass their weaknesses, so no student should ever give up!

What Is an IQ Test?

In school, kids with learning problems often take intelligence tests (IQ tests). *The most common IQ (Intelligence Quotient) test is called the WISC-R. It is made up of many small tests that measure different functions or abilities. Half of them are called Verbal Tests because they have a lot of language in them. The others are called Performance Tests. The performance tests do not have as much language in them; they use more spatial and other visual and motor abilities.* A student may do much better on the Verbal or on the Performance Subtests depending upon his or her intelligence specialties. Some students show big differences in how they do on the different parts of an intelligence test. Those students may have the most specialized brains!

IQ tests are usually given by psychologists who figure out a total score after you take the test. An average IQ score is 100. Above 100 is above average, and below 100 is below average. However, IQ tests are not perfect measures of intelligence. They show how you did in specific areas on the day you took the test. This means that scores can vary somewhat each time you are tested. Also, there are many things these tests don't measure. They don't measure how creative you are, how good you are at inventing things or at thinking up new ideas. They don't measure your attention or social skills very well. They don't check on how organized you are, how hard you can work, how well you can recall several things at once, or how good you are at understanding brand new concepts. Nor do they measure many important language skills, some other key parts of mem-

Some people take IQ tests too seriously. In this picture, one girl is very pleased because she found out that her IQ is 120, while the other girl is disappointed to have an IQ of 119. Really, the girl on the left is over-valuing her score, and the one on the right should not be so sad. IQ tests are not perfect measures. There are many important abilities (and disorders) that are not measured on IQ tests. They give you only a general idea about your abilities or intelligence.

ory, or your ability to use good learning strategies. But IQ tests can help people understand some things about your style of learning.

What Is an Achievement Test?

Achievement tests are given often in schools. *They measure your skills in subjects like reading, spelling, arithmetic, and writing. They may also test your vocabulary, your ability to look things up, and other skills that are needed for school.* Different schools use different achievement tests. Most of the time, achievement tests are taken by groups of students all at the same time every year or every other year to see how much progress everyone is making. Sometimes a student with learning problems is tested alone, outside the classroom.

In either case, a series of scores is figured out. You and your parents and your teachers are sent a report that tells how you did. You might be told that your reading comprehension is at a certain grade level. For example, your reading comprehension might be at a 6th grade, 6th month level. That means that you can understand what you read as well as any average kid in the 6th month of the 6th grade. If you are in fourth grade, the score just named would make you look like an excellent reader. On the other hand, if you are in the eighth grade, you would be two years behind in reading!

Sometimes the scores are also reported in percentiles. You might be told that you are in the 50th percentile in your overall mathematics abilities. That means that 50% or half of students at your grade level are better at mathematics than you are, and 50% are worse at mathematics than you are. If you are in the 90th percentile, it means that only 10% of students did better than you did on the test. Sometimes there are different kinds of percentiles. National percentiles tell you how well you did compared to everyone else in the country. Local percentiles compare you to other kids who live where you do. Also, if you go to a private school, your results might be reported in independent school percentiles which compare you to other students who go to private or independent schools.

Like IQ tests, achievement tests are not perfect. There are many things they don't measure. They don't test how original your ideas are. They may not be very good at judging your writing ability. Also, since most achievement tests are multiple-choice tests, the students who are great at multiple-choice questions may get very high scores. There are also some kids who are "disasters" when it comes to multiple-choice tests. They just don't like to be forced to choose among several answers on a test. Some would much rather think up their own original answers! There are other students who know the answers, but they work too slowly and can't go fast enough on achievement tests. Also, there are kids with attentional problems who do poorly on achievement tests because they keep putting answers down in the wrong column; they have trouble focusing on many details at once. So, like other tests, achievement tests can help your school and parents to understand you better. But to understand a student really well, it is necessary to look not just at the achievement tests but also at how that student does on a lot of different tasks in school every day.

What Is an Evaluation?

Many students with learning problems have to have evaluations. *This means that they get tested by one or more experts in learning disorders.* The purpose of an evaluation is to find out exactly what a student's learning problem is and to come up with ideas for working with that student in school and at home. In the United States, there is a law (Public Law 94-142) that schools follow for evaluating children with learning problems.

Sometimes an evaluation is called *multidisciplinary.* This means that you are evaluated by a team of people. Each team member has a different specialty connected with learning and behavior in school. The team might include a physician, a psychologist, a language therapist, a social worker, and a special educator. Each person tests you, examines you, looks over your schoolwork, or talks to you or your parents to get an idea of how you are performing. Usually, the team has a conference, and they put together all of their ideas about you and come up with a plan. This plan includes the kinds of help you will get in school. Evaluations are done either in school or in clinics or offices. If the evaluation is done outside school, its results are used to help the school, your parents, and you.

Whether you have an evaluation done in school or out of school, you need to have a good understanding of the results of that evaluation and the plans being made for you. Every student has to become familiar with his or her strengths and weaknesses. As we have said over and over again in this book, if you don't understand yourself, it will be almost impossible to help yourself! If there are parts of an evaluation that are confusing to you, you need to ask and keep asking about them until you feel sure you understand everything on the evaluation. Don't be shy when it comes to finding out about yourself.

Should You Tell Your Friends about Your Learning Disorders?

It is a good idea to tell your friends at least a little bit about your learning disorders. Many kids do this, and it never seems to cause any problems. You might say to a friend: "You know I have some learning problems. I've had these checked out, and they found out that I'm not stupid or anything like that, but I have some small learning problems that get in the way at school. That's why I have to get some tutoring. It's not a big deal, and I'm still able to be good at a lot of things." Finding the right words can be difficult, but if you don't tell your friends the truth, they might start to imagine much worse things about you. Even if you don't tell them anything, they'll find out sooner or later that you're having some problems in school. You're not going to lose any real friends by being honest!

What If You Feel Embarrassed about Getting Help at School?

There are many students who feel embarrassed about getting tutoring or any other special help in school. More than anything else, they just want to be like everyone else. They don't want to look unusual or special in any way. Being in a special class for learning disabilities, going to a resource room or tutor, or visiting a guidance counselor may make them feel too different (even weird). Also, they are afraid that other kids will notice and that those kids may say something mean or call them names because of their problems with learning. This can be scary.

Nobody likes to feel embarrassed. Nobody likes to get called names. But if you need help, you need help. It doesn't make sense to refuse help because it's too embarrassing. If you don't get help, you'll get even further behind in school. Sooner or later, when you're extremely far behind, other kids will notice that. Then, they might insult you anyway. If anyone questions what you're doing while you're getting help, you can just say that you're trying to get ahead in reading or that you're getting some help so you can write better or do math better. If you explain your learning disorder to your friends as we suggested in the preceding section, they may be able to give you some assistance. They could talk to kids who make fun of you and get them to stop.

If some kids continue to give you a hard time, you need help from an adult. You should discuss the situation with your parents, with your teacher, and, if necessary, with the principal or head of the school. Sometimes it's helpful if a teacher explains learning disorders to the whole class (without mentioning your name). If you are being teased too much, don't try to fix the problems all by yourself. That usually doesn't work.

What Do People Mean When They Say That a Kid Is Poorly Motivated?

A lot of times when a student has learning disorders, people say he is "poorly motivated." *Often when a teacher or parent says this, he or she means that the student doesn't try very hard or has given up completely.* To be motivated toward something is to want very much to accomplish it or get it. Usually, students are motivated if there is a goal that they like. You might be motivated to learn algebra in school if you really like mathematics, especially if you think algebra is fun. You might be motivated to get good grades in school if you enjoy success and if you like having your friends and relatives tell you how smart you are.

While it's true that almost everybody would love to get good grades, there's more to motivation than simply wanting them. You get motivated only if you think you really have a chance of getting what you want (like good grades). If you think you have no chance of getting what you want, even if you try, you lose your motivation. Another part of motivation has to do with how hard it would be to get something. If you think that you could possibly get good grades but that it would take super-human effort—too many very hard long hours for you to get those good grades—you might lose your motivation because all that effort would not be worth it to you.

So a student can lose motivation because he doesn't like a

goal, because he feels he could never get that goal, or because the goal would be much too hard to get. You can see how a student with learning disorders might lose motivation when it comes to getting a good report card. If motivation is too low for too long, it becomes a problem because you learn to feel helpless. You feel as if things just happen to you, and it doesn't make much difference what you do. Eventually that feeling can make you extremely unhappy.

How Do You Know If You're Lazy?

There is probably no such thing as a lazy kid. A kid may *look* lazy if he or she has lost motivation. Some kids look lazy when they really have attentional difficulties that make it extremely hard for them to concentrate. A lot of other kinds of learning problems can make someone look lazy when really she isn't. For example, a kid may seem lazy because she hates getting started on homework. She has to be reminded about six times before she begins to do something like a report. Her parents think she's lazy, but she really has a fine motor problem that makes writing a huge chore, so she just dreads getting started.

What If You're Bored in School?

School should not be boring. A really active, alert, and interested mind can find exciting things in a lot of subjects and activities. Even if a teacher keeps repeating things over and over again, you can use the repetition to come up with new concepts and new ways of using what you've learned. *Most of the time, when kids are bored in school, it is either because they are having trouble with their attention or because they don't fully under-*

stand what is going on. Also, it is easy to get bored when you're sad or anxious. Sometimes students use boredom as an excuse for not concentrating. They say they don't concentrate because they are bored, but it may be that they are bored because they can't concentrate.

What Do You Do If You Have a Brother or Sister Who Gets Much Better Grades in School Than You Do?

It's not unusual for a kid with learning disorders to have a brother or sister who is an awesome student. This can create real problems.

Sometimes adults—parents, grandparents, or others—say things like: "Why can't you be like your brother? He works so hard and gets *all* of his work done. He gets such good grades. You're just as smart as he is; how come you're so lazy?" Adults who say such things can make you very angry at your brother or sister who does so well in school.

You might also feel jealous, and sometimes even think that you hate the brother or sister who is "so perfect" all the time. This can cause fights. *Actually, arguments and fights among all brothers and sisters are common; in fact, they are normal. They are sometimes referred to as sibling rivalry. However, when one member of a family is much more successful than another, tension can get too high. Then, the relationship needs to be worked on, or it will make everyone unhappy.*

The following list will give you some suggestions about what to do if your brother or sister gets better grades than you, and the situation is causing problems for you. After you read the list, you may come up with some more ideas of your own to add to it.

First of all, try to explain to the adults who keep comparing you to your brother or sister that no two kids are alike. (As we know, sometimes adults don't fully understand a kid's learning disorders.) You should point out that you have many things that you do very well and that you are not in some kind of contest with your sister or brother.

Try to develop areas of interest that are totally different from those of your brother or sister who does so well in school. For example, if your brother is on the track team, you might try to play tennis. If your sister plays the piano, you could play the drums or start collecting rocks. In other words, try never to compete directly with your brother or sister. You should find ways of feeling good about yourself without competing.

Try not to add too much fuel to the fire. If you insult your brother or sister, she or he is going to find ways to make fun of your learning difficulties.

From time to time, you need to have a talk with your brother or sister. Be honest about how you feel. Explain your learning disorders. Try to find a good moment—a time when you are getting along well—to do this. Try to get your brother or sister to work *with* you to help you deal with your problems.

If your brother or sister keeps making fun of you because of your learning problems, you should ask for a family discussion about the matter. Your parents might insist that your brother or sister stop making cruel comments. It is never appropriate to embarrass someone, especially when that person has a problem.

Try to arrange some private time with your parents. Having your brother or sister around all the time that you're with your parents encourages competition.

Tell your parents you would like them to deal with your school problems in private—not in front of the whole family.

Don't lose all interest in school just because you think you will never do as well as your brother or sister. Remember, it is not unusual for a kid who had tremendous problems during the earlier grades to start doing very well later on. You will never improve if you decide not to "keep a head" in school because your brother or sister is getting much better grades.

What If Your Parents Hassle You Too Much about School?

Many students with learning problems complain that their mothers or their fathers worry about them too much and hassle them too much about how they do in school. They are annoyed when a parent criticizes them or forces them to do homework. Kids need to realize that it would be much worse if their parents didn't care at all about how they did in school. *A parent who puts pressure on a son or daughter is actually showing that child one very special kind of love. But even if that pressure is a kind of love, it can still be extremely annoying. A kid and his parents need to negotiate.* They need to decide just how much pressure and just how much arguing about school is the right amount.

Some parents try to help or tutor a son or daughter, and this sometimes leads to major battles at home. Often it is better to have someone outside the family do the tutoring. This could be a professional tutor, a neighbor, or an older kid who is a successful student. If there is constant arguing over schoolwork, then it is probably a good idea for the whole family to meet with someone who can offer advice, someone who understands school and family problems.

The following is a list of ways in which you can use a parent to help you in school.

1. A parent can help you talk with a teacher or principal if you're having trouble getting along with a teacher.

2. A parent should not do your homework for you; however, she or he can help get you started.

3. A parent can set up certain rules at home to improve your work habits. For example, there can be a certain time each night for quiet brain work. During this period, the whole family should be quiet (although not silent) and be doing quiet work during that time each evening.

4. A parent can help organize a home office for you. If you have trouble concentrating, it is probably not a good idea for you to work in your bedroom. Bedrooms are often the hardest places to concentrate. You also may need to change work places a few times while you are working.

5. A parent can help you check over your work to make sure you've done it correctly.

6. A parent can be available if you have any questions.

7. A parent can help you look up things or use a library.

8. A parent can help you brainstorm or think up ideas for a report or a project.

9. A parent can talk to you about your school problems. She or he can help explain test results and things the teacher has said about you. A parent should try not to keep secrets about school from you.

10. A parent can help you get the help you need in school.

11. A parent can play games with you to help you remember math facts, spelling, definitions, or other things you need to be able to retrieve from your memory for school.

So, you can see that it is important for a mother or father to be helpful without overdoing it. If you think your parent or parents are putting too much pressure on you, you need to discuss this with them. Try to save that discussion for a peaceful time, when no one is angry at anyone. You need to sit down and talk about the kinds of help a parent should give you and the kinds of things that you should do by yourself. Sometimes you need to show adults that they can trust you.

What Does It Mean To Be Depressed?

Some kids with learning problems get depressed. *To be depressed is to be too sad.* Sometimes depressed students are sad because they have not had enough success in school. Nothing seems to go well for them. They feel terrible about their schoolwork. They feel that they have disappointed their parents, their teachers, their friends, and themselves. Often, kids who are depressed seem to lose interest in everything. They get tired

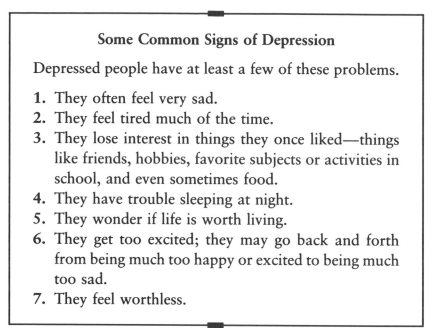

Some Common Signs of Depression

Depressed people have at least a few of these problems.

1. They often feel very sad.
2. They feel tired much of the time.
3. They lose interest in things they once liked—things like friends, hobbies, favorite subjects or activities in school, and even sometimes food.
4. They have trouble sleeping at night.
5. They wonder if life is worth living.
6. They get too excited; they may go back and forth from being much too happy or excited to being much too sad.
7. They feel worthless.

easily. They get moody and they feel worthless. They may find that they are sleeping more, that they are spending more time doing nothing and wanting to do nothing. When a kid feels that he or she is getting depressed, it is time to get help. Many things can be done to rescue someone from depression. The sooner a depressed kid gets help, the better.

Some students are not really depressed but they are anxious. They have a lot of anxiety. They get very nervous or scared before a test or when they are called on in class or even when they are invited to a party. A certain amount of anxiety is normal. Everybody gets anxious sometimes. But it's a problem if you're too anxious or if you panic too much of the time. These feelings can lead to depression, which is a bigger problem, of course.

What Is Self-Esteem?

Do you respect yourself? Do you have confidence in yourself? Do you think that you are as smart or as good looking as other kids? If your answer to these questions is "yes," you probably have good self-esteem. *Self-esteem has to do with what you think of yourself.* Some students have excellent self-esteem. They feel good about the way they are. They feel happy about the future. They feel hopeful. They feel in control of what happens to them. Other kids have a shortage of self-esteem. They feel kind of worthless a lot of the time. They believe everybody else is better than they are. It is possible to have low self-esteem in only one area. For example, some kids have low self-esteem in school but feel good when they're playing sports or joking around with friends. But others have no self-esteem in any parts of their lives. As you can imagine, if you have low self-esteem in all areas for a long time, you can get depressed.

A good way to increase self-esteem is to spend time doing things you do well and enjoy, activities that make you feel smart or strong or talented, things that help you respect yourself and receive respect from others. Then keep congratulating yourself on your accomplishments! But if you think your self-esteem has been dropping too fast or for too long, then it's time to get some help from someone you can trust and respect such as a parent, your doctor, a clergyperson, or someone at school.

What Is Counseling or Therapy For?

Some kids with learning problems can get help through counseling or therapy. They talk with someone like a counselor, psychologist, or psychiatrist. This kind of help is especially ap-

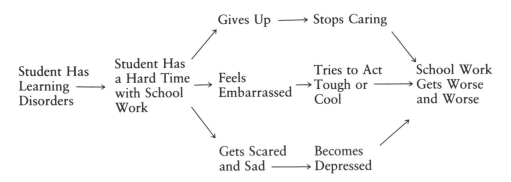

The diagram above shows three dangerous pathways that might be taken by students who have learning disorders. In the top pathway, a student gives up, stops caring, and probably stops working. In the middle pathway, a student gets so embarrassed that he or she needs to act extremely tough to cover up. The toughness naturally interferes with day-to-day work in school. The bottom pathway is one in which a student becomes very frightened about some learning problems and then goes on to become depressed. The depression then adds to the learning disorder to make schoolwork even worse. Students who are on one (or more) of these pathways often need help to find better ways of coping with their learning disorders.

propriate if learning disorders are making a student feel sad, and the sadness is interfering with learning and life in general.

Some students with learning disorders develop behavior problems too. They act tough or "cool" or disruptive to cover up their learning disorders so that other kids won't notice that they're having trouble with school. A kid may be so busy acting cool or tough that he or she begins to neglect schoolwork. Then the student gets further and further behind so that it becomes very, very hard to catch up. The diagram shown above describes the wrong pathways that kids with learning disorders can follow. These dangerous pathways make a learning problem much worse than it needs to be. Kids may need advice or counseling to get off the wrong pathway and onto a better one.

Sometimes a whole family needs to meet with someone who can help them work on their problems. If you need counseling, it does not mean that you're crazy or weird. It just means that you need a chance to work things out, to get to know yourself better, and so get some good advice on how to handle your problems. *Again, it is better to get help with problems when you're young than it is to let the problems get worse. Then they can cause even bigger troubles later on in your life.*

Why Do Some Kids Take Medicine To Help Them in School?

Some students improve in their learning or behavior when they take certain medicines that are prescribed by a doctor. Most of the time, these are stimulant *drugs.* They are usually given for problems with attention. The most common drugs are Ritalin, Dexedrine, and Cylert, although sometimes others are used. These medicines don't make a person more intelligent. They don't usually improve reading comprehension or mathematics skills. But they do help some students concentrate better and be less impulsive.

In a way, these drugs are similar to coffee. Coffee is also a stimulant; it wakes up most people so they can be more alert and "tuned in." The chemicals in stimulant drugs are similar to a chemical, caffeine, found in coffee. Some students who have real trouble concentrating, who "burn out" too easily in class, seem to strengthen their focus with the medicine. When this kind of medicine is used, it has to be prescribed by a physician who has to see the student from time to time to check on how things are going, to examine him or her, and to make any necessary changes in the amount of medicine the student takes.

Medicine is never the whole answer. It should be combined with a student's own effort, with teachers and parents who understand the problem, with work on identified learning disorders, and with any other needed advice and help. All of these things together can improve attention. Some students get embarrassed about taking medication. They don't want anyone else to know that they take pills to help them concentrate. If you do take medicine, your classmates don't have to find out. You should have your privacy. However, it is probably a good idea for the teacher to know that a student is taking medication.

What Is an Organizational Problem?

There are some students who have a lot of trouble in school because they are disorganized. These kids are said to have organizational problems. *There are many different kinds of organizational problems. For example, some impulsive kids do everything too quickly and too carelessly. But there are two other common kinds of organizational problems: one has to do with space, and the other with time.*

Students who have spatial organizational problems have a lot of trouble keeping track of things. They keep losing everything. They have trouble finding a pencil, a piece of paper, or a place to sit when they want to do their homework. Pages keep falling out of their notebooks, which are a mess. They lose books, assignments, and personal possessions. They just can't seem to remember where they left things. Plus, their lockers and their bedrooms often look like dumps! One boy described his

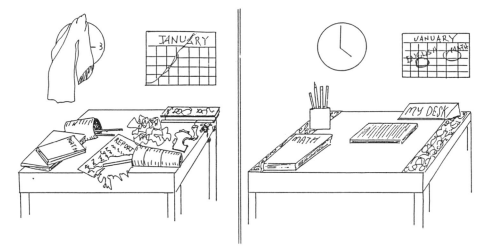

Some kids are very organized and some aren't. In the picture above, you can see desks belonging to two different kids. The desk on the left belongs to someone who has real trouble organizing space and organizing time. He's covered up his clock and he is not making much use of his torn calendar. This student probably forgets to hand in assignments and loses many important possessions. He doesn't even finish his sandwich! On the right is a very neat desk, one belonging to a student who is obviously well organized in space and in time.

locker as a "black hole." He said that nothing that's gone into it has ever again come out!

Other students have trouble organizing time. They get mixed up about sequences and time. They are often late. They can't remember when an assignment is due. They don't know how much time to allow themselves to complete an assignment or job. They never are quite sure what to do first, what to do second, and what to do third when they write a report or work on a project. Time is just plain confusing for them. They can't manage time, and this makes them disorganized.

How Can You Fix Organizational Problems?

To fix an organizational problem, you need to understand that you have the problem. Then you need to design all kinds of tricks to help yourself. Some schools give you help with organization. They have courses on study skills. They teach you about making up schedules to help you manage time. They also teach you about doing things in the right order when you work on a project or report. They teach you techniques for organizing your ideas and thinking. These include outlining, underlining, taking notes, and arranging a notebook. They might also help you organize your desk, develop a filing system for important papers, and set up work schedules.

Someone helping you get organized might also teach you how to study for tests. This might include deciding what to study, how to study, and how to test yourself to see when you think that you know enough to stop studying. Organizational problems can be some of the hardest problems to fix, but if you are aware of your organizational problems, you can combine the suggestions of others with your own ideas to improve yourself.

What If You Have a Lot of Problems Taking Tests?

Some students with learning disorders do poorly on tests, even when they think they "know their stuff" before a test. It's as if they have a test-taking jinx! But, most of the time it's *not* just bad luck—there's a good reason for their disappointing and embarrassing test scores. *Most kids who repeatedly do poorly on tests don't stop to figure out where or how they went wrong.*

There are some common reasons why students have a hard time with tests, so the next time you do badly on a test (and everyone does some of the time), consider the following possibilities.

 You didn't think about your memory while you studied. Some kids are sure they'll remember things if they understand them. As we have seen (in Chapter 3), you can understand something without remembering it. When you study, you need to think about your memory and about what you are learning, and you need to be checking up on how well your memory is storing the information.

You didn't use good study methods. The methods you use for studying have a lot to do with your test results. A poor score may just mean poor preparation. For example, some kids never test themselves when they study. You should use test results to decide how you need to change your study strategies in the future. A way of studying your test results is presented on pages 277–278.

You didn't study long enough or hard enough. Sometimes kids get bored or have trouble concentrating while they study for a test. You may do badly because you just don't think hard enough or long enough while preparing for a test. You need to work out ways to make your concentration stronger so you can register facts and skills more deeply in memory. To do this, you may need to take notes, underline, reread, whisper what you're reading while you read, make lists of key words, or ask yourself questions.

You fooled yourself. Sometimes it is hard to admit to yourself that you don't really understand something, so when you study you just ignore or skip over hard things that confuse you. But, if luck isn't with you, those hard ideas appear on the test the next day. You tried to pretend you knew the stuff, and you could fool yourself but *not* the test. Try to catch yourself fooling yourself. Get some help with confusing ideas or facts.

You felt too cocky or overconfident. It is possible to feel too sure of yourself during a test. Then you might work too fast, make careless errors, and decide that you don't need to check over your answers. Many good students say they think it is good to be just a bit scared or tense while taking a test; being a little uptight makes them more careful.

You studied the wrong things. There are students who have trouble predicting what will be on a test. They keep studying the wrong things. Kids like that need to practice answering questions made up from material in the book. Sometimes it is good to talk to a friend (who is good in a particular subject) about what will probably be on the test.

You didn't really understand the questions or instructions on the test. Some students don't take the time to understand exactly what is being asked for. Others have a language disorder that makes it hard for them to interpret questions. In either case, it is important to go over questions and directions carefully, sometimes even underlining key words or phrases with a pencil. Also, never try to follow directions after reading only part of them. Read every word carefully.

You often have trouble with a particular kind of test. Kids with writing problems often find essay tests a real pain. Other kids keep scoring low on multiple-choice tests. Several answers on a question look pretty good to them, and their minds can't stand having to narrow down the choices. For example, a reading comprehension test may ask for the best title for a paragraph. A really bright kid may read the paragraph and think of her own title. Because she thinks her idea is so much better than any of the choices given, she can't concentrate on picking the best answer from among those offered on the test. She keeps doing poorly on such questions, even though she's a very good reader. A girl like that (and anyone else who has trouble with a particular kind of test) needs practice with the questions that cause trouble. Sometimes a student may need to ask a teacher for another way to show what she or he knows. A kid who does poorly on multiple-choice tests may have trouble with tests for getting into college. He may need to have a school counselor or someone else notify colleges that the results of the test do not show his abilities accurately.

You made a lot of careless mistakes. Some kids hate checking over their work, especially on tests. So, they make many silly mistakes. If you have time during a test, you should go back over everything before you hand in your paper. (Work that is not timed like a test should always be checked over.)

You ran out of time. Pacing yourself is crucial during a test. Before you answer any questions, look over the whole test and decide how much time you have for each part or each question. Don't spend too long on one question or problem, especially if it seems too hard. Do all the easy things first and come back to the tough ones later. Don't forget to keep one eye on the clock so that you won't fall behind. Some kids who take tests very slowly need to be given more time. Some kids, when they take tests to get into college (the SATs), have a problem working fast enough. Such students can get permission to take the tests untimed.

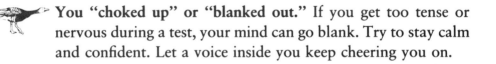 **You guessed too much.** Sometimes it's good to guess when you don't know an answer, but other times it is better just to skip the question. What you should do depends upon a couple of things. First, you should find out from the directions or from the person giving the test whether giving your best guess is a good idea. Second, you should consider whether your guess is an intelligent one or simply a wild one.

You "choked up" or "blanked out." If you get too tense or nervous during a test, your mind can go blank. Try to stay calm and confident. Let a voice inside you keep cheering you on.

You gave up during the test. You shouldn't have.

How Can Computers Help You Do Better in School?

Many students with learning problems get help from computers. *A computer is especially good for writing.* It can make up for some weak fine motor skills that may make your handwriting hard to read. When you do a report on a computer, it looks neat. A computer also gives you an extra memory. It won't make your ideas any better, but it can help you organize them, and it may help with spelling, punctuation, and grammar. Some kids with learning problems are able to use educational software to help them with spelling, mathematics facts, and reading skills. Such software is worth investigating.

$$\frac{1}{8} + \frac{3}{16} = \frac{5}{16}$$

$$\frac{4}{5} \times \frac{1}{2} = \frac{2}{5}$$

$$\frac{9}{11} \div \frac{9}{10} = \frac{10}{11}$$

A computer can be extremely important for helping a kid who has some learning problems. It can also help a kid overcome the effects of a fine motor problem (so that his or her writing will be neat). There is computer software that can help certain kids learn some basic skills (like math facts and word decoding). Therefore, kids with learning disorders need to become very skilled and comfortable with computers.

What Is Creativity?

Creativity is the ability to come up with original ideas. Many kids with learning problems are creative. They have awesome imaginations. In fact, they seem to be better at forming their own ideas than they are at using other people's ideas.

There are many different ways to be creative. You can be creative in drawing, in telling stories, in daydreaming, in inventing things, or in thinking up new ways of solving all kinds of problems. Every kid needs to understand the ways in which he or she is creative. You need to use your creativity to keep up your self-esteem, to develop some "products"—like artwork, stories, or models—that other people will admire. The worst thing is to waste creativity, to have it in you but not to use it to get the praise you deserve for it. Creativity as a concept is very closely related to brainstorming, which we discussed in Chapter 5.

We hope that this chapter has answered some of your questions about learning disorders, about yourself, or about other people you know. It may make you think of other questions too. In the next chapter, we will look to the future and think about what happens to kids with learning disorders as they go through school and grow up.

CHAPTER NINE

What's Ahead

TONY'S STORY

Since his earliest years in school, Tony's had severe learning disorders that have interfered with every subject. He had trouble learning to read. No one could read his writing. He was always a poor speller. Although he got tutoring, he was forever behind in mathematics. He had an evaluation in school that showed that he had language disorders, fine motor problems, some difficulties with visual-spatial thinking, and a little trouble with his attention.

For a long time, Tony had trouble believing that he simply had learning disorders. He kept wondering whether he was really retarded, and thinking that maybe people were not telling him the truth about himself. Finally, when he was in seventh grade, Tony was able to understand, accept, and even talk about his learning disorders. At that time, he also became aware of his strengths.

The most amazing thing about Tony is that he never gave

up. He is tough, and from the beginning he was determined to make it in school. Tony was always popular, and he was a good—but not great—athlete in several sports. Tony's soccer coach said that he was about the hardest-working player he had ever seen. He practiced every day and got the most out of his abilities because he never surrendered. He was willing to risk failure even in sports where he wasn't very good. Such behavior is typical of Tony.

Tony's learning problems were at their worst in junior high school. He did poorly on tests in almost every subject. His teachers liked Tony, but they were frustrated by him. They wanted to keep him back in eighth grade, but he insisted that he wanted to be promoted. He said that he was working hard and trying hard and that he didn't think it was right to be "punished" publicly for his learning disorders. He said keeping him back would only discourage him and that he would be extremely embarrassed if he had to repeat eighth grade. Tony went to the school principal. He said to his parents, "I want to stand up for my rights." Tony was very good at speaking up for himself. He also was excellent at knowing how to use adults to help him. He was never ashamed about getting help. The principal was impressed; the school decided to promote Tony to ninth grade.

High school seemed to be easier for Tony. He took courses he liked a lot. Gradually, his writing and reading improved because he never stopped practicing. However, he continued to have some problems in math, and he also had trouble learning a foreign language. Because he had worked so hard at soccer, he had become a first rate player. He was the varsity goalie in his sophomore year. During high school, Tony got very interested in computer science. He liked making his own software, which was very impressive. He got A's in two computer courses.

Tony got into a very good college on a soccer scholarship. He majored in computer science but also took a lot of courses in English. He actually was enjoying reading and writing. Last year Tony graduated from college, and he got an excellent job. His boss recently promoted him, saying, "Nobody works as hard as Tony." Needless to say, Tony's parents are really proud of him.

Recently, Tony went back and visited his junior high school. The teachers remembered him. They remembered how they had wanted to keep him back in eighth grade and how Tony insisted that he could do ninth grade work if they would believe in him. He felt very glad that they had agreed to believe in his ability to succeed without repeating eighth grade. The teachers said that they also were glad that they had decided to believe that Tony could do it. Tony really enjoyed showing his former teachers how successful and happy he had become as an adult.

Thinking More about Tony

Try answering the following questions after reading Chapter 9.

- What traits did Tony have that helped him become successful and happy?
- How was Tony helped by playing soccer?
- All kids with learning disorders are not like Tony. What do some kids do that actually harms them when they have learning disorders?

THOUGHTS ABOUT THE FUTURE

Someone who's had a hard time in school might begin to wonder about the future. Such a person could easily ask, "If school has been so hard, will everything I do be hard? Will I have just as much trouble with my work when I grow up? Will I ever be able to learn anything very well, go to college, or get a good job? Was I born to struggle forever?" These are important questions. Many kids think about them; others try hard *not* to think about them because such thoughts about the future frighten them.

Feeling Good about the Future *and* the Present

This chapter will help kids prepare for the future. Looking ahead can help students make things go well for themselves both now and later. Throughout this entire book, kids have been encouraged to feel good about themselves and what's ahead for them. This final chapter will review some things that we hope will be especially useful.

People Who Succeed and People Who Don't

It's important for kids to realize that there are many famous people who had learning disorders when they were in school. In just about every field today, there are women and men who had trouble learning to read, who found spelling very difficult, who had terrible writing problems, or who were always behind in mathematics. On the next page, you'll find a list of a few such people. This list should show you that it is possible to be a great athlete, a famous inventor, a successful businessperson,

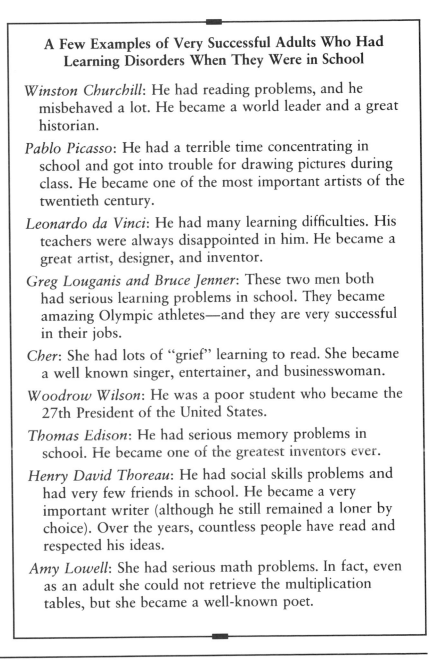

A Few Examples of Very Successful Adults Who Had Learning Disorders When They Were in School

Winston Churchill: He had reading problems, and he misbehaved a lot. He became a world leader and a great historian.

Pablo Picasso: He had a terrible time concentrating in school and got into trouble for drawing pictures during class. He became one of the most important artists of the twentieth century.

Leonardo da Vinci: He had many learning difficulties. His teachers were always disappointed in him. He became a great artist, designer, and inventor.

Greg Louganis and Bruce Jenner: These two men both had serious learning problems in school. They became amazing Olympic athletes—and they are very successful in their jobs.

Cher: She had lots of "grief" learning to read. She became a well known singer, entertainer, and businesswoman.

Woodrow Wilson: He was a poor student who became the 27th President of the United States.

Thomas Edison: He had serious memory problems in school. He became one of the greatest inventors ever.

Henry David Thoreau: He had social skills problems and had very few friends in school. He became a very important writer (although he still remained a loner by choice). Over the years, countless people have read and respected his ideas.

Amy Lowell: She had serious math problems. In fact, even as an adult she could not retrieve the multiplication tables, but she became a well-known poet.

or even the president of a country after a pretty slow start in school.

By the way, we could also make a list of grown-ups who never succeeded in their jobs or careers, even though they were great students when they were young! So when you look around your school and see some kids that you think are real "brains," keep in mind the possibility that a student with learning problems might end up being much more successful as a grown-up than a student without learning problems. Some people succeed when they're young, while others do much better during their grown-up years. Of course, some people succeed both as children *and* as adults.

Adult Life Compared to School Life

In many ways, it is easier to be a grown-up than it is to be a kid in school. For one thing, there are more ways to be successful. When you grow up, you're allowed to practice your specialty, to do "your own thing." You can go after jobs that you're good at and spend as much time as possible getting stronger in your strengths. You also can avoid many of the things that are your weaknesses or that embarrass you. For example, if you're not very good at writing, you can pick a job or a career that has very little writing in it. If you like working with engines or building and fixing things, you can select an occupation that allows you to do these things most of the time. Also, when you grow up, you have more privacy. You are less likely to be criticized in front of the people you work with than you are to be criticized in front of your classmates, friends, or brothers and sisters.

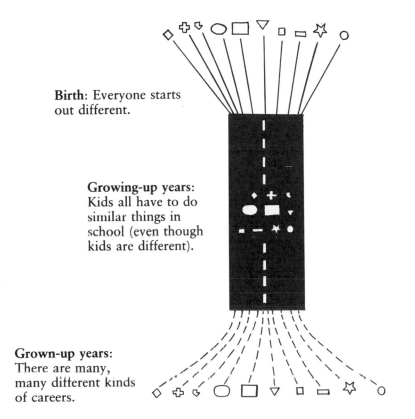

Birth: Everyone starts out different.

Growing-up years: Kids all have to do similar things in school (even though kids are different).

Grown-up years: There are many, many different kinds of careers.

Everybody starts out in life different from everybody else. We all have different strengths and weaknesses from the moment we are born. All of us with our different kinds of brains are then required to go to school and learn pretty much the same things. Later, when people grow up, they can pursue many different kinds of careers and interests. So, if a kid is having a hard time in school, she can look forward to adult life when she will be able to "do her own thing."

What To Do Now

Even though you may look forward to a successful life as an adult, you can't just sit back and wait for those years to arrive. You have to work while you're in school, and sometimes you will have to do things that you don't do very well. There's a

The boy in this picture is dreaming about his future. This is a kid who really likes cars. He thinks about the possibility that he might be fixing cars someday. He could even start his own automobile repair shop. Then maybe he could sell cars and own his own dealership. Eventually he would like to design his own cars. Who knows? He could even have a car named after him! It doesn't matter what you are interested in; if you keep your hopes up and preserve your ambitions, you can do great things.

reason for this. It is so that you can improve your weak areas (even though your performance may embarrass you at times).

You should think of school as being like a ladder that you climb because every step up the ladder prepares you for adult life. If you try to skip too many steps, you may fall down and hurt yourself and never reach the top. The ladder is particularly hard to climb for students with learning disorders. They keep slipping and wondering if the effort is worth it. These students should remember that by doing a lot of different things they can learn more about their own strengths, weaknesses, and interests.

Kinds of Success

It's important for students, as well as adults, to remember that success can occur in many ways beyond school and work. These include the ability to be happy in general, to do well in family relationships, to enjoy other people, to help them, and to be part of the city or town where one lives.

USING THE PRESENT TO PREPARE FOR THE FUTURE

There are proven ways that kids with learning disorders can make the school years less embarrassing, more fun, more successful, and a better preparation for adult life. The following pages will explain some ways to do this.

Understand Yourself

One of the biggest mistakes made by students with learning disorders is that they keep trying to fool themselves. This is one of the worst things to do. Many students with reading problems, attention deficits, or trouble with mathematics make believe they have no problems at all. Maybe they think that if they ignore their troubles, their troubles will disappear. That never works. Instead, in order to improve, a student must admit that he or she has learning disorders.

It is also important to understand exactly what the learning disorders are all about. For example, if you have an attention deficit, you really need to understand what an attention deficit is, what kinds of problems it is causing, what might help and what might make things worse, and how there can be some good things about attention deficits.

If you are having trouble in school, and if you don't understand that you have a learning disorder like an attention deficit, you might think that you are crazy, dumb, or just plain lazy. Not only that, you won't know what to do about it, so you may begin to feel helpless and useless. Some kids with learning disorders think that somehow their brains were not made for school. As you might guess, kids who have this kind of belief are in for some really hard times during the school years (and maybe even afterwards).

Make Sure That the Adults in Your Life Understand Your Situation

Not only do you need to be certain that *you* understand your learning disorders, but you also need to make sure that the adults who live and work with you also have an understanding of you. This can be very tricky. Suppose you have a language disorder and that you are getting help from a tutor to improve your reading and writing skills. But suppose also that a particular teacher doesn't know that you have a language disorder. Because she doesn't know about your problems, she keeps calling attention to your errors; and she says you are careless with your grammar when you write reports. She also unintentionally embarrasses you by calling on you in class. Since it's hard for you to think up and express ideas quickly enough to answer questions in class, the other kids sometimes laugh.

This teacher needs to know about your language disorder. Then she can change her approach in order to help you, which is what she wants to do most of all. You or your parents or your tutor needs to have a talk with the teacher. Many teachers know very little about learning disorders. They may not really understand what a language problem or an attention deficit is because they are not specialists in these areas. Sometimes it is up to a student and his or her parents to help a teacher understand. One of the reasons teachers become teachers is that they like kids. They don't want to hurt you. In order to help you, they need to understand you and your needs.

Sometimes your parents may have trouble understanding your learning problems. You can try to teach them as well. You might also want your parents to talk to your tutor or to a school counselor or psychologist. You might even show them parts of this book.

Don't Use Your Problems As an Excuse To Avoid Work

Once grown-ups understand your learning disorders, you need to realize you can't use your problems as a "cop-out." You can't blame everything on your learning disorders. Adults expect you to be working on your problems, to be improving steadily. They need to understand you, and sometimes they should even feel sorry for you. But they can never let you act like an invalid or cripple. You can't go up to your teacher after class and say: "I don't think I should take that test tomorrow. I have a sequencing problem. Kids with sequencing problems should not have to take tests." That just won't work. Everybody has to assume responsibilities, even students who have learning disorders that make work more difficult. People have to understand how tough things are for you, but they also need to know that you are working hard and that you are not using your problems as a way of avoiding work. Besides, most kids don't want to seem different. They want to do what other kids are doing.

Work On Getting Teachers To Like and Respect You

One of the most important things you can do when you have learning disorders (and even when you don't) is to work hard on building strong relationships with your teachers. To get the best possible education, you need to be liked and respected by those who are teaching you. It takes effort to develop a trusting relationship with a teacher. The teacher will do some of that work, but the student needs to do his or her part.

Teachers are human. They have feelings similar to yours. They need to know you respect them and the job they are doing. They need to feel good about their relationship with you.

The following are some things you can do to build strong relationships with teachers and to get them to like and respect you.

Realize that different teachers have different ways of teaching and different personalities. You can't adore every teacher, and your teachers won't all treat you the same way. It can be hard to adjust to the differences among teachers, but you need to work on it. When you grow up, you'll have to be good at working well with many different kinds of people.

Act friendly. It is important to greet your teacher, to look him or her straight in the eye while having a conversation, and to say some socially nice things when you meet a teacher in a corridor, cafeteria, or elsewhere.

Try to visit alone with each of your teachers. Arrange to see each one from time to time just to talk about how things are going. This could be done after school, during lunch hour, or at other times. These meetings do not need to be very long, but they should take place with every teacher you have.

Share your true feelings with your teachers. Let them get to know you. Tell them about things that you like to do, about things at home, and about relationships you have with your friends. Often, teachers can give you excellent advice and understanding.

When you're having trouble in a subject, it is very important for _you_ to make an appointment to see your teacher. You should ask your teacher what you can do to improve. You also should ask your teacher why she or he thinks you are doing poorly. Then you can offer your explanation for the problem. Let your teachers help you.

 Try to let the teacher know that you are working on any learning disorders you have. Teachers are disappointed when they think a student is using learning disorders as an excuse for not working, or when they think a student with learning disorders is not trying to help himself or herself at all.

Let the teacher know when you are truly interested in something covered in class. You might say: "It was neat studying about robots. I hope we can learn more about things like that."

Every once in a while (at least), try to do more than you are asked to do. Show the teacher that you are really interested and that you are really willing to take on some extra work. Keep listening and thinking about what is going on in class and try to discover some ideas that you think are especially interesting. You should be doing your extra work with those ideas. Sometimes it is hard to find any exciting ideas, but you need to keep searching until you do find them.

Let the teacher know when you think he or she has done a really good job of teaching you. Say things like: "I really learned that stuff well when you made those diagrams on the board."

If you want, every so often you can write your teacher a note telling her or him how you are feeling about the class. Some kids prefer writing to talking.

Encourage your parents to go to meetings at school. It can help your relationship with a particular teacher if your mother or father communicates with that teacher.

Try not to be irritating. It is pretty easy to tell what kinds of things you or other students do that definitely annoy a teacher. You need to get to know each teacher you have to find out the kinds of things that irritate him or her. Then you can concentrate on avoiding those behaviors. For example, most teachers hate students to talk out of turn, disrupt things, make jokes at the wrong times, show no interest, or fall asleep during class.

Remember, building good relationships with many kinds of people is an important part of life in general. When you finish school, you will have to build relationships with your bosses. If a boss doesn't like you, you could run into big trouble with your job or career. It could really wreck your life if one boss after another doesn't like you. Therefore, start practicing now; work on relationships with teachers. (Top students are usually great at this.) You can probably think of ideas to add to the list you've just read.

Strengthen Your Strengths

Sometimes kids with learning problems think of themselves as one big mess of deficits, disorders, disabilities, and weaknesses. They forget all about the things they do well. Don't let that happen to you. Always think about and work on what you do best. If you are good at drawing, get even better at drawing. If you are good at a particular sport, practice especially hard at

This boy is using his excellent artistic ability. He realizes the importance of getting better and better at the things he does well. At the same time, he is getting help with his mathematics and reading skills because he is weak in these areas. No matter what happens, he won't stop strengthening his strengths.

that sport. If you are a talented dancer, perfect your dancing. A student who is having a lot of trouble in school desperately needs to be doing *some* things really well in order to get recognition.

A student who does not seem to do anything well will suffer from something called *chronic success deprivation*. You and the adults in your life cannot let this happen to you. One way to prevent it is to develop a specialty. When a kid gets very interested in something and starts to get really good at it, the kid's brain may be sending the kid a clue that this "something" is his brain's specialty. The brain may also be sending a clue about the future, about what the kid might do well as an adult. It would be a shame to miss such clues or notice them but then do nothing about them.

Report Cards—Which is Better?

READING	A
SPELLING	B+
MATH	C
WRITING	D
ART	D
PHYS. ED.	C−

READING	C
SPELLING	D
MATH	D
WRITING	C
ART	A
PHYS. ED.	B+

There are many different ways to be successful. The report card on the left is that of a student who is really good at reading and spelling but not so good in writing and art. On the right is the report of a student who is struggling with spelling and math, doing okay with reading and writing, and excelling in art. No one can say that one of these students is "smarter" than the other. No one can really say that one has more ability than the other. We can only say that one has a different kind of ability from the other. There is no one course in school that can tell you whether you're "intelligent" or not. This is because there are so many different ways to be intelligent.

Know When and How To Bypass Your Weaknesses

One important way to improve in school is to know when and how to avoid using your weaknesses. You avoid using weak abilities by having bypass strategies. Bypass strategies are the ways that you get things done without letting your learning disorders interfere too much. Sometimes you can figure out and use a bypass strategy all by yourself. Sometimes it is your teacher who thinks up a bypass strategy for you. There is no end to the different kinds of bypass strategies that a student can use in school. Once you understand your learning problems, you can invent excellent bypass strategies.

The following is a list of some examples mentioned in earlier parts of this book. It should remind you of things to think about.

1. **Using a word processor for writing reports.** A word processor is like an extra memory. Kids who have some memory problems might find that a word processor really improves their ability to write, even though it doesn't fix up their memory problems—it just bypasses them.

2. **Using a calculator in mathematics class.** Students with some problems in math sometimes find it helpful to use a calculator to do math problems. A calculator does a lot of the memory work and frees up a person's mind for problem solving and other kinds of thinking. Some mathematics teachers do not like this particular bypass strategy. A student needs to ask permission to use it.

3. **Dictating your best ideas into a tape recorder before you write a report.** Many students with writing problems have trouble thinking and writing at the same time. It's better if

they think first and then write. Using a tape recorder can bypass the problems that students have with thinking and writing at the same time.

4. **Having a teacher call on you only for questions that can be answered with a "yes" or a "no."** Some students with language problems have real trouble participating in class discussions. When they are called on, they just can't think up the right words and put their ideas into sentences fast enough. It can be very helpful for a student with that kind of language disorder to have an agreement with the teacher that he will be called on in class only for questions he can answer with a "yes" or a "no."

5. **Sitting close to the teacher.** Many kids with attention deficits find that the farther back in the classroom they sit, the more likely their minds are to wander off and daydream. For this reason, a good way to bypass their attentional difficulties is to sit up front. Also, kids with attention deficits need to be active. They may need to take frequent breaks to get up and walk around. They may also need to keep their hands in motion. One way to do that is to become a very good note taker. That can keep a student busy *and* help him or her listen.

6. **Making diagrams and charts while reading.** There are many students who have trouble remembering what they've read. For example, they have difficulty taking a test the day after reading a social studies chapter. Some of these students have a weak memory when it comes to language and reading material. However, many of them are very good at visualizing things, so they can bypass their language memory prob-

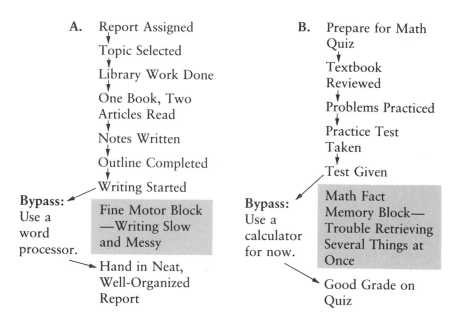

A. Report Assigned
→ Topic Selected
→ Library Work Done
→ One Book, Two Articles Read
→ Notes Written
→ Outline Completed
→ Writing Started

Bypass: Use a word processor.

Fine Motor Block —Writing Slow and Messy

→ Hand in Neat, Well-Organized Report

B. Prepare for Math Quiz
→ Textbook Reviewed
→ Problems Practiced
→ Practice Test Taken
→ Test Given

Bypass: Use a calculator for now.

Math Fact Memory Block— Trouble Retrieving Several Things at Once

→ Good Grade on Quiz

C. Science Test Announced
→ Chapter Read
→ Chapter Understood
→ Practice Questions Tried

Bypass: Use visual memory. (Make diagrams, charts, pictures to study.)

Verbal Memory Block

→ Excellent Test Results

Each diagram above illustrates how a student can use a bypass strategy to work around a learning disorder or "block."

lem by making a lot of diagrams and charts while they read. They then can study these visual materials and remember them much better than they would if they depended only on words and sentences.

Being a good strategist means stopping and thinking before doing something—thinking about the best and easiest way to solve a problem, write a report, or study for a test. Some kids with learning disorders have no bypass strategies at all. They just plunge into things. Sometimes these kids are impulsive, but not always. Other kids are afraid to use bypass strategies because they think that using them will make them seem too different—even weird or abnormal. They want to do just what everyone else is doing. The truth is that, most of the time, other students don't know and don't care if a bypass strategy is being allowed for one of their classmates. It's very important for students with learning disorders to remember that one way to improve in school is to become an excellent strategist.

Stand Up for Yourself

Students have rights. Students with learning problems have the same rights as other students, and maybe a few more. For example, a student has the right not to be unnecessarily embarrassed in class. If something that your teacher does causes you embarrassment, you should speak to him or her about it. You have a right to be reasonably comfortable in your classroom. It is possible to say to a teacher or a principal that you think you have a right not to be embarrassed. Sometimes, your parents can help you represent your rights in this respect.

When decisions are made about your future, you have a right

to understand these decisions and why they were made. You also have a right to express your opinion about the decisions. For example, if it is decided that you should be kept back in seventh grade, and if you do not want to be—if you think it will make you very embarrassed and depressed—you should say so to the adults in your life. If you feel strongly about it, you need to say it strongly. You have a right to be heard. This does not mean that decisions will always go your way. But you need to feel that your point of view is being taken very seriously, that it is making a strong contribution to the final decision.

There are good and bad ways to stand up for yourself. It is not a good idea to yell or use bad language in front of the teacher. Remember, teachers also can get embarrassed. They, too, are human. You will find it easier to stand up for yourself if you form strong relationships with your teachers. Get them to like you. Get them to trust you. Talk to them after class. Show them you are trying and that you are interested in what they are teaching. In Chapter 7 we talked about all of the skills you need to make friends. You need many of those same skills to make friends with your teachers. Develop them and use them.

Whenever it's possible, read some of the reports and evaluations that have been written about you. You should try to understand as much of what is written about you as possible. You should also feel free to disagree with something in a report and to let people hear your point of view.

You may also need to stand up for your rights at home. Most kids seem to have no trouble doing this! However, even at home, you have to be gentle, fair, and respectful. A lot of shouting and anger doesn't work. It's a good idea to find a quiet and peaceful time to negotiate with a parent about homework or other rules. Try to have important discussions at times when everyone's in a good mood and not in the middle of a battle.

Don't Be Afraid To Get Help If You Need It

There are many people who are especially trained to help students with learning problems. As we said in Chapter 8, you have to be able to overcome any embarrassment that you might feel about getting help. Sometimes that takes a lot of courage. Below, you will see a list of the kinds of people who help students with learning problems. You can see that the list is quite long. In some schools and in some towns, more of these kinds of people are available than in other schools or other towns. Your parents can usually find out about what's available where you are. Often, the students who improve the most are the ones who know how and when to get help from the experts. Kids who pretend they don't need help seem to get worse.

Some Professionals Who Help Kids with Their Learning Disorders

Tutors (sometimes called Educational Therapists): They can help you catch up in many subject areas. They can also help you understand your learning problems and develop strategies to deal with them.

Remedial Reading Specialists: They can help you improve your decoding and comprehension skills in reading.

Classroom Teachers: They can help a lot in making it easier for you to learn, especially if they understand the nature of your learning disorders.

Psychologists: They can help you understand your learning problems as well as your personal problems.

Psychiatrists: They can help you deal with family problems and with your feelings. They can also prescribe medicine to help you.

Social Workers: They can help you work out problems you are having in school and in your family.

Speech and Language Specialists: They can help you improve your language skills.

Occupational Therapists: They can assist you in developing better motor skills.

Special Educators: They can provide special teaching methods.

Neurologists: They, along with pediatricians, can take a close look at how your nervous system is working and at any problems related to it.

Guidance Counselors: They can give you advice about what subjects to take in school, what to do when you're finished with school, and how to cope with the stresses and strains of everyday life in school.

Advocates: They can represent your rights as a student.

Pediatricians and Family Doctors: They can often help you understand your learning problems and also deal with health issues as you grow up. Doctors will sometimes prescribe medication to help with attention and learning. Some pediatricians actually specialize in helping kids with learning disorders. They are called developmental pediatricians (like the author of this book).

School and Clinic Nurses: They can give you good advice about health problems that might be affecting your learning.

> **Others:** Believe it or not, there are many other kinds of professionals available to help kids who are struggling in school.

Learn from Your Mistakes

Some of the best lessons you can learn come from tests and reports *after* they are returned to you from your teacher. At that point, you should spend a lot of time thinking about what went right and what went wrong on an exam or report. Look carefully at each mistake and try to decide why it happened. Doing this is, in a way, like being a doctor who diagnoses problems, treats them, and tries to prevent them from occurring again. The box that follows gives you a method for figuring out your performance on a test. For additional suggestions about what to do if you have problems taking tests, you can look back at Chapter 8 of this book.

> Below is a list of possible reasons for making mistakes on a test. After getting back a test, look over your mistakes and ask yourself which of the following is true. (You can use the abbreviations given after the statements to mark your test paper.)
>
> 1. I made a careless mistake. (Attention—ATT)
> 2. I never studied that. (Planning—PL)
> 3. I knew it, but I forgot it on the test. (Memory—MEM)
> 4. I didn't really understand that "stuff." (Comprehension—COM)
> 5. I didn't really understand the question. (Comprehension of Question—CQ)

> **6.** I didn't use the right way to solve the problem or figure out the answer. (Problem Solving—PS)
>
> You may want to get some help using this checklist.

DON'T GIVE UP

Whatever you do, don't surrender—"keep a head in school." Some students do surrender because they decide that trying takes just too much effort. They believe that they will never succeed anyway. It's as if they leave their heads at home in bed. Many of these students are afraid of embarrassment. Some develop behavior problems. Because they believe that they will never get recognition for their school work, they look for other ways to be recognized. They may act tough or extremely "cool." They think that acting this way will prevent other kids from noticing that they are not "keeping ahead" *or* "keeping a head" in school.

Some students who give up on school keep criticizing it. They say that school is worthless and boring. They say it has nothing to do with anything important or anything that interests them. They blame the school, the teachers, and the subjects for all of their problems.

Students who give up on school often find other kids in town who have also given up on school. All of these kids together form strong cliques or gangs. They get a lot of pleasure from impressing each other. This is because they don't seem able to impress anyone in the adult world. As we saw in Chapter 7, it is certainly important to have friends and to be part of a group.

But it's a problem to be a slave to a group. As great as it may seem to be accepted in a group, it can mean that you may feel heavy pressure to base your whole life on doing and saying whatever will please the rest of the group.

SET GOALS AND BELIEVE YOU'LL REACH THEM

Students with learning disorders need to be able to think big. They need to be able to see themselves as getting what they want out of life. It is always important to spend some time and thought looking ahead to what you would like out of life. You need to dream about these things, and you need to believe that your dreams will come true. This is called having optimism. Be optimistic and ambitious. If you do not aim very high, you will never get very much. If you try for many goals, you'll reach at least some of them. It is also important to encourage yourself. In Chapter 4, we mentioned that inside you there is a voice that should be cheering and rooting for you. You need to keep that voice cheering. Also, you need to take some good risks, even the risk that you may fail. You'll never succeed if you don't risk failing. Although everyone gets discouraged from time to time, you shouldn't be discouraged for very long. Keep setting goals that are high and goals that are fun. After all, having exciting goals is one important way of "keeping a head in school."

Important Words and Phrases

Abstract Concept (129*). Something you can think about but cannot ever touch or feel. Abstract concepts would include democracy, fair play, evaporation, and creativity.

Active Working Memory (70). The ability to hold in your mind several different parts of a task while you are working on it. For example, while writing a report, it is important to remember the topic, the ideas you want to include, and the length the report should be. Someone with an active working memory problem might "lose the topic" from her mind while she is busy writing the report.

Amnesia (50). A condition in which someone loses part of his or her memory.

Anxiety (240). A feeling of being afraid. Students who feel a lot of anxiety are often very nervous about school, about friends, or about things going on at home. Anxiety may be very specific (such as a fear of taking tests) or it may be so general and vague that a kid feels a lot of fear without really knowing what she or he is afraid of. Everybody has some anxiety, but when it becomes extreme, you need help from an adult.

Association (77). A process through which ideas, words, or visual images get attached to each other in your mind. You might form an association between someone's face and his name, between a song and its title, or between a word and its definition.

Attention (20). A brain process (sometimes called concentration) through which you are able to focus your thinking, your sensations, and

*The number in parenthesis shows you the page in the book where you can find this term.

281

your memory so that you are not trying to do or think about too many things at one time. People with strong attention are said to be very *selective*. They concentrate on the right things at the right time.

Automaticity (70). The ability to recall a fact or a skill very quickly and with very little effort or attention. For example, you might be able to tell time or tie your shoe laces and remember how to do those things so easily and fast that you don't really have to think very hard while doing them. As you go through school, more and more of what you learn in the early grades needs to be remembered automatically so you can think about other things while you are remembering them. If you have to stop and think about how to make an *H*, you will have a hard time writing book reports!

Basal Ganglia (8). Bunches of nerves in the middle of your brain that work closely with the cerebellum to make your muscle movements smooth.

Basic Skills (148). The abilities that you need to get through school. Many basic skills are acquired during elementary school. They include the ability to add, subtract, and multiply as well as the ability to read, write, and spell.

Body Position Sense (114). Knowledge of where in space your arms, legs, and trunk are at any given time. Your eyes, as well as nerves in your muscles and joints, keep track of this. Sometimes they need to work very quickly, such as when you are involved in running, jumping, or doing calisthenics. People with poor body position sense are clumsy; they are likely to fall a lot. They may have trouble balancing themselves and playing certain sports.

Brainstem (6). The lower part of your brain that connects with the spinal cord. It controls many functions you don't need to think about, such as breathing, coughing, and keeping your heart going at the right rate.

Brainstorming (136). The ability to think up your own ideas or to put together facts in your own way to create your own ideas. You might brainstorm to come up with ideas for a short story, for a science project, or for some interesting things to do next weekend.

Bypass Strategies (270). Methods that can be used to work around a weakness. For example, a student with a language disorder may try to learn visually. A kid who has trouble controlling a pencil may learn to type or use a word processor as a way of bypassing the pencil control problem.

Categories (64). Groups of things or ideas that go together. For example, fruits, furniture, and sports all represent different kinds of categories. Each includes many things that have certain characteristics in common. For example, the category *fruit* would include apples, oranges, and pears.

Central Nervous System (5). Your brain and your spinal cord.

Cerebellum (7). An area located at the back of your brain. It helps to regulate all kinds of muscle movement.

Cerebral Hemispheres (8). Two halves of the brain that look very similar and are joined together by millions of nerve fibers. They are where you do your thinking, interpret incoming information, and get your muscles to start moving.

Chronic Success Deprivation (268). A condition in which a student goes through many years of life with few, if any, real triumphs. A kid who is not very popular, who has school problems, and who doesn't play sports well may be deprived of success in life at that point. Sometimes a student like that just gives up or gets very depressed.

Code Switching (211). The process through which a person talks differently to different kinds of people. You might use one sort of language to speak to your best friend and a very different kind of language to talk to an adult whom you've never met before. You probably would not speak to your grandmother or grandfather as you would to your teacher. The ability to switch from one code to another is an important social skill.

Concept (124). An idea that describes a group of other ideas or associations that usually go together. For example, the concept of meat includes bacon, steak, hamburgers, and ham. Sometimes a concept can fit into other concepts. Thus, the concept of meat itself is part of a concept called food. As you go through school, concepts become more and more abstract, and there are more and more concepts inside concepts! Good students have an excellent understanding of the concepts they encounter from day to day.

Concrete Concept (130). An idea that describes things you can see or feel. The concept of dessert includes a variety of possibilities that you can see.

Conformist (213). A person who says things, does things, and acts just like everybody else. A student who is a conformist may be afraid to be different. He or she may talk like other kids, dress like other kids, and spend all day long trying to be as "normal" as possible. That student may lose all his or her individuality.

Context Clues (154). Hints about word meanings that you get while you are reading. You get these hints by understanding *other* words in the sentence.

Decoding (152). The process in which a person looks at a word and figures out its pronunciation and meaning.

Depression (239). Feelings of extreme sadness and anxiety. A student who suffers from depression is likely to lose interest in every-thing. He or she may be tired all the time, get into very sad moods, and feel worthless. Kids with depression need to get some help to bounce back and feel better about life.

Depth of Processing (57). The strength with which information is reg-istered in memory. If someone tells you something, and you are not listening very carefully, the information may not get very far into your memory. If, on the other hand, you are listening very carefully because it is very important for you to remember it, the information, in a sense, goes in farther; it has more depth of processing, and it is more likely to be remembered.

Distraction (22). Something that interferes with paying attention to what you are concentrating on. For example, a clock in a classroom may distract you from listening to what the teacher is saying.

Elaboration (67). A process in which someone takes an idea and adds other thoughts or facts that help to make the idea more mean-ingful.

Episodic Memory (69). The ability to recall details having to do with things that have happened in your life time. Your episodic mem-ory might help you recall what you did last summer or who you sat next to on the bus during a field trip a few months ago.

Expressive Language (85). The ability to put your own ideas or feelings into words and sentences.

Eye-hand Coordination (168). The ability to get your vision and your fine motor function working together. For example, if you are copying a map from a book, you need to interpret the shape of the map visually and use that information to guide your finger movements on the paper. You even need good eye-hand coordination to trace the map!

Fine Motor Dyspraxia (121). A condition in which someone cannot get the right muscles to move in the right order to accomplish a task. Someone with a fine motor dyspraxia can picture letters (if he or she has a good motor memory for letters), but that person cannot get the muscles to form the letters properly. Somehow it is too hard to translate a plan of the motor action into the precise muscle movements.

Fine Motor Skill (113). The ability to organize and regulate the small muscles (especially in the hands). Fine motor ability allows you to do things like build models, draw pictures, and type.

Finger Agnosia (118). A dysfunction in which someone does not know where his or her fingers are in space without actually looking to see where they are. As you write, your fingers report back to your brain. Your brain can then instruct your fingers where to go next as they form letters. People with finger agnosia have trouble keeping track of where their fingers are in a letter during writing. For them, writing is often a very slow and difficult task.

Frontal Lobes (9). Parts of your brain located right behind your forehead. They control your judgement, your behavior, and some of your emotions. They are also important for guiding your attention. The back part of the frontal lobes contains the motor cortex.

Grade Level (229). The grade in school in which a student's skill would be average. For example, if you were in 5th grade and your reading comprehension was at a 6th grade, 6th month level, you would be ahead in reading; in other words, you would be reading as if you were an average student in the middle of 6th grade, even though you were in only 5th grade.

Gross Motor Skill (113). The ability to get your muscles working together in the right way to accomplish tasks or activities that you do with your arms, your legs, or your whole body. Gross motor ability allows you to be good at sports, for example.

Hyperactivity (34). A tendency to move around too much. Some kids (but not all) with attention deficits tend to be a bit "hyper." They are on the go all the time. They have trouble sitting still without fidgeting. Remember, though, there is nothing wrong with being hyperactive if your activity accomplishes a lot each day. It is only when the activity is wasted that hyperactivity becomes a problem.

Hypothalamus (8). Part of the brain that helps to control appetite, thirst, body temperature, and some feelings (including anger).

Impulsiveness (25). A trait that makes some people do things or say things too quickly and without thinking. A student may get into trouble in school for saying something in class she should not say. If she says it very quickly without thinking about the consequences, she is acting impulsively. Someone who does an assignment quickly, without much planning, could also be considered impulsive.

Inferring (95). A process through which someone uses "clues" to figure out meanings or adds information to what another person is saying or writing. For example, suppose a teacher says: "I want you all to be very well prepared for class tomorrow." You might infer that he expects you to go over your notes and your text very carefully and that he might be giving you a quiz the next day, even though he has not said any of these things.

Insight (135). A thought that comes to you and clears up some confusion or lack of understanding. You might get an insight into how electricity goes through a wire or why some kids act like bullies.

IQ (227). A measure of intelligence based on a test. Most often students take a WISC-R test to determine their IQ (Intelligence Quotient). The IQ score is based on how well you did on the test *for your age*. An IQ of 100 is average for your age. The entire IQ test is made up of short tests that measure verbal and non-verbal abilities. IQ tests do *not* check out all important abilities, so a kid can be much smarter than his or her IQ test shows!

Language Disorders (96). Conditions which cause people to have trouble understanding words and sentences, or communicating through words and sentences. A language disorder might affect only your ability to understand or only your ability to speak or both. A language disorder interferes with learning to read or with expressing ideas in writing.

Learning Disorders (2). Weaknesses in specific functions that make it hard for kids to get skills and knowledge fast enough in school. Kids often have several learning disorders which together make school very difficult.

Mathematics Facts (185). Knowledge that you need to learn in order to use various operations in mathematics. Mathematics facts include the multiplication tables, basic addition (such as $5 + 2 = 7$), and basic subtraction (such as $7 - 2 = 5$). These facts eventually need to become automatized, because, for example, if you are to be good in algebra, you must be able to remember your multiplication tables automatically.

Mathematics Operations (184). Processes in which you apply math facts to solve problems. Operations include such processes as long division, the calculation of percentages, and the solution of algebraic equations.

Motivation (233). The drive and desire to be successful or to accomplish something. Students with good motivation have a strong feeling that they want to do well and that they can put forth the effort to do well. Students lack motivation if they are not interested in being successful, if they feel that trying to succeed will take more effort than they are able or willing to put out, and sometimes if they feel that they cannot succeed.

Motor Action (114). A muscular activity that you do intentionally. Combing your hair, copying down an assignment, or petting your dog would all be examples of motor actions. Tripping, rubbing your nose, or turning over while you are asleep would not be considered motor actions because you did not really plan those activities.

Motor Coordination (115). The ability to get the right muscles to work in the right order to accomplish a motor plan. Someone with poor motor coordination may be very awkward when trying to do certain things. It is possible to have poor fine motor coordination (which could affect something like handwriting) or poor gross motor coordination (which would affect one's ability in sports like basketball) or both.

Motor Cortex (11). The parts of the brain (in the back of your frontal lobes) that get muscles to move. When you decide to throw a ball, for example, the motor cortex gets the action going. It gets help from the cerebellum and basal ganglia, which makes the movements smooth. Nerves in the spinal cord connect with nerves going out to muscles so that those muscles get the message and can complete the motor action.

Motor Memory (119). The ability to recall the right sequences of muscle movements needed to accomplish motor actions. You need motor memory to remember how to make letters. You also need motor memory to recall how to ride a bicycle or drive a car.

Motor Plan (115). A "blue print" or preview of what a motor action will be like. For example, someone trying to kick a football may picture in his or her mind what the different steps of kicking the ball will actually look like. That image is a motor plan.

Non-Verbal Concept (128). A group of ideas that go together and are easier to picture in your mind than they are to describe. For example, to understand what a fraction is, it might be easier to picture a pie that is being sliced up than it is actually to try to describe fractions in words. Other non-verbal concepts might include triangle, "out of bounds" in sports, or miles per hour.

Occipital Lobes (11). Parts of the brain at the back of your head that interpret and make use of visual information.

Operations (184). These are processes that are needed to accomplish certain tasks. In mathematics, the operations include multiplication, division, and subtraction.

Oral Dyspraxia (121). A problem knowing what muscles of the mouth, tongue, and jaw to move, and in what order, to pronounce certain sounds or words. Someone with an oral dyspraxia may mispronounce words or sound very hesitant when he or she talks.

Parietal Lobes (10). Parts of the brain that are near the side of your head. They control how you interpret sensations; they are the "feeling" part of the brain. They interpret information coming in from places like skin, muscles, and joints.

Percentile (sometimes called percentile rank) (229). The number of students out of every one hundred who perform less well than a particular student. Percentiles are often used to show results of achievement tests. If you are in the 75th percentile in reading, that means that 74 out of every one hundred students are not able to read as well as you can.

Procedural Memory (69). The recall of different skills or processes that you use. In your procedural memory, you store methods for brushing your teeth, for doing addition problems, and for signing your name.

Reading Comprehension (154). The ability to understand language as it is presented in writing. Good reading comprehension is necessary for figuring out newspaper articles, stories, and textbooks.

Recall (68). The ability to remember something that has been stored in your long-term memory.

Receptive Language (85). The ability to understand ideas that are conveyed in words and sentences. Your receptive language ability enables you to interpret explanations and directions.

Recognition Memory (68). The ability to identify something as familiar or "right" to you. For example, you might see somebody at a store and realize that you have seen that person before; your recognition memory tells you that she is someone you know, even if you can't retrieve her name.

Reconstruction (55). The process of picking out, rearranging, and shortening information to fit it into short-term memory.

Registration in Memory (52). A process through which new information first gets put into your short-term memory. If somebody tells you a telephone number, you remember it by registering it in your memory as the person is telling it to you.

Rehearsal Strategies (76). Techniques that can be used to make it easier to plant ideas deeply in short-term memory. For example, some students form pictures in their minds while they are studying a science or social studies chapter. Others may whisper important ideas under their breath to help remember them.

Self-monitoring (26). Watching what you are doing to make sure it's going according to plan. Self-monitoring lets you be sure that you are on the right track, that you are doing what you are supposed to be doing the way you are supposed to be doing it. Checking things over is an example of self-monitoring. Behavior or making friends can also involve self-monitoring. If you are talking to a friend and you notice that he or she is looking at you in a strange way, you should try to monitor what you are saying. You might discover that you are saying things that are making your friend angry. Because you have self-monitored, you can start saying something different so your friend will feel better about you.

Sequencing Ability (110). The capacity to understand and remember information that comes into your mind in a particular order. Sequencing ability helps you use the order of days of the week or months of the year. It helps you remember your schedule of classes or activities. You may remember all the things on your schedule, but if you get them in the wrong sequence or order, you'll never be anywhere at the right time.

Sequential Memory (59). The ability to remember things in the correct order, such as the digits in a telephone number or the steps in a series of directions.

Sight Vocabulary (152). The number of words that you can recognize the instant you see them.

Social Feedback Cues (207). Hints that you get from other people that tell you how you are doing socially. For example, by looking at the expression on someone's face or listening to the tone of that person's voice, you might be able to tell whether he or she likes what you are saying or doing.

Social Language (209). The words and sentences that someone uses while being sociable. For example, it is possible to talk in a way that sounds "cool" or to use language that somehow comes across as "weird" to other students. The words you choose, the tone of your voice, and the kinds of sentences you create make an impression (either good or bad) on other people.

Sound-Symbol Association (151). The knowledge that specific sounds go with specific visual symbols (groups of letters). By forming sound-symbol associations, it is possible to look at written words and pronounce them. That, of course, is critical for reading out loud.

Spinal Cord (6). A long thick tube that goes down your back and contains various nerve connections that enable you to receive sensations and to make muscles move. The spinal cord is connected to your brain and it gives off nerves that go out to your skin, your muscles, your joints, and some of your body organs.

Stimulant Medicine (44). A kind of medication that is sometimes used to help kids who have trouble with attention. The most common stimulants are Methylphenidate (Ritalin), Dextroamphetamine (Dexedrine), and Pemoline (Cylert). These medicines are not tranquilizers; they don't really "calm your nerves"; they don't make you smarter. They just wake you up more so you can focus better.

Strategies (76). Techniques or methods that are used to make work or learning easier. For example, taking notes during a lecture might be a good strategy to help you remember important points.

Summarization Skill (156). The ability to shorten and retell in your own words something you have heard, experienced, or read. As you go through school, it is increasingly important to be able to summarize well. You may need to summarize a story or a chapter for a report. After a math class, you should be able to summarize the most important material from the lesson in order to prepare for a quiz.

Syntax (93). The order of words in a sentence. Syntax is an important part of language. As kids go through school, they come to realize that the order of words has a big effect on the meanings of sentences.

Temporal Lobes (11). Parts of the brain at the sides of your head just behind the frontal lobes. The temporal lobes have many jobs, including the interpretation of language. There is also a lot of memory stored in the temporal lobes.

Thalamus (8). A kind of relay station that gets sensations (all except smell) from the rest of your body and helps to send them to the correct parts of your brain so they can be interpreted and used properly.

Topic Maintenance (211). Knowledge of how long to talk about a subject. To know just how long to talk about something, so that people don't get bored or tired or think you're strange, is part of being good at "the social game."

Topic Selection (211). The choice of something to talk about. Knowing what to talk about (and what *not* to discuss) when you are with certain people or in a certain place is an important social skill.

Verbal Concept (128). A collection of ideas that go together and are easy to think about in language. For example, the concept of friendship might include being nice to other people, having close friends, and not being alone all the time. Friendship is a concept that can be best described in words. For most people, it would be harder to think about friendship in pictures than it would be to describe friendship in words.

Visual Memory (59). The process through which sensations coming in through your eyes get remembered. For example, you are likely to use your visual memory to recognize somebody's face if you've seen that person before.

Visual-Spatial Ability (108). The capacity to figure out information that enters the brain through your eyes. Visual-spatial information tells you about the positions of things in space, about shapes and how they differ from each other, and about the sizes of objects. Visual-spatial ability allows you to tell the difference between a small *b* and a small *d*.

Word-by-Word Reading (153). Oral reading that's too slow and doesn't flow smoothly. Usually a person who reads word-by-word reads with little or no expression. Such a student often has not yet developed automatic word recognition. Sometimes the student works so hard to say the words properly that he or she misses their meanings.

About the Author

Dr. Mel Levine is a pediatrician who specializes in school-age children and teenagers who are having problems with learning or with school in general. For more than twenty years, he has been trying to understand learning disorders and working with students to help them overcome their problems.

Dr. Levine grew up on Long Island, New York. For the most part, he enjoyed school, but he had some hard times. In kindergarten, he was near the bottom of his class, partly because he had trouble using a scissors properly (he still does), and also because he always crossed over the lines when he colored. Despite this slow start, he succeeded during the earliest grades of school. He did run into some trouble in fifth grade when he couldn't seem to get organized, failed to hand in assignments, and didn't get along with his teacher. He was almost left back that year, but he didn't think he should be, and his parents agreed with him, so he continued on and improved slowly but surely.

Athletic activities were a problem for Dr. Levine. He wasn't very good at playing most sports, and he was often picked last when kids were choosing up sides. In baseball, they put him far out in right field where the ball would almost never arrive. This might have been boring, but he had always loved animals, and there were excellent toads and salamanders in right field! In junior and senior high school, Dr. Levine got very good grades and did well in activities other than sports. For example, he became editor of his high school newspaper.

After graduating from high school, Dr. Levine attended Brown

University in Providence, Rhode Island. He liked college and did well there. During his college summers, Dr. Levine worked as a camp counselor and helped teach boys and girls how to climb mountains. At that time, he became very interested in how different kids reacted to the challenge of steep hills and hard work. After Brown, Dr. Levine was selected to be a Rhodes Scholar at Oxford University in England.

Dr. Levine had decided to become a doctor when he was eight years old, so when he came back from Oxford, he went to Harvard Medical School. After medical school, he was an intern and a resident at The Children's Hospital in Boston, and then a pediatrician in the Air Force on a large base in the Philippines. That job also included being the school doctor. Working with teachers and kids in school was something Dr. Levine considered important and found interesting.

When he got out of the Air Force, Dr. Levine again was a pediatrician at The Children's Hospital in Boston where he ran many clinics, some of which were designed to help children with learning problems. He became particularly interested in students who were basically smart but who were having trouble learning and working in school.

Dr. Levine has developed various tests that are used to help doctors understand kids who are having learning problems. He also has written many books and articles on the subject. Presently, Dr. Levine is a professor of pediatrics at the University of North Carolina School of Medicine. He directs its Center for Development and Learning, runs various clinics, does research, writes articles and books, evaluates kids, and teaches doctors, teachers, and other kinds of people to help students with learning disorders.

Dr. Levine's home is called Sanctuary Farm. There, he and

his wife raise about twenty-five kinds of geese. For twenty years, Dr. Levine has studied these animals—their nutrition, their behavior, and their individual learning styles. He likes the geese because they are very smart, very funny, very tough, and very individualistic—no two are exactly the same. Sanctuary Farm is also home to forty pheasants, seven swans, three horses, four dogs, and too many Maine Coon cats to count. There are also two mules who are excellent at learning but who have serious problems with their social skills.